# Simple Steps to Option Trading Success

### BY JIM GRAHAM AND STEVE LENTZ

### FOREWORD BY JON "DR J" NAJARIAN, PTI SECURITIES

MARKETPLACE BOOKS
COLUMBIA, MARYLAND

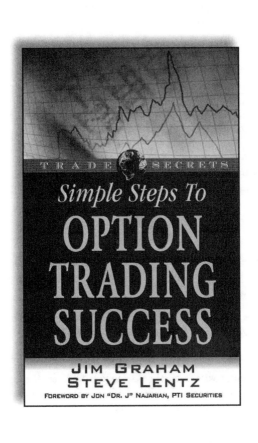

TRADE SECRETS

*Simple Steps To*

# OPTION
# TRADING
# SUCCESS

## JIM GRAHAM
## STEVE LENTZ

FOREWORD BY JON "DR. J" NAJARIAN, PTI SECURITIES

ISBN 1-59280-054-8

*Printed in the United States of America.*

# Contents

# Simple Steps to Option Trading Success

# Foreword

Investors have had plenty of reasons to be angry in recent years. Corporate scandals. Outrageous executive compensation packages. The dot.com dive. Tainted analysis. Shameful behavior by corporate chieftains. Even outright fraud perpetrated by trusted professionals that have bankrupted companies and robbed unsuspecting investors of their capital. Many who had stacked their portfolios heavily on the equities side saw large portions of their retirement savings evaporate in the huge market decline. We all felt the pain.

But I believe two very positive trends have resulted from the recent cycle of events. First, I am confident investors are more receptive to investment vehicles like options that can reduce the risk from a severe market downturn. And, it is my profound hope that everyone involved in the markets—from the casual investor to the active trader—will exercise more discipline and craft a solid game plan *before* putting their hard earned dollars on the line. When the prudent, risk-balancing benefits of options are combined with a rigorous investment plan, every investor has a solid shot at profiting in the market whether it's soaring to new heights, trending flat or declining.

Describing options as a "prudent" market play may come as a surprise to many who perceive them as risky business suitable more for high-end speculators. But in reality, options can, and should, play an integral role in balancing a portfolio. They allow you to keep your risk exposure to a level you can personally live with, and enhance your overall return on investment. They're an amazing tool once you've learned how to select and apply the right option strategies to meet your personal investment goals.

I've been trading for over two decades. I've been a market maker, a floor trader, and a trading instructor. I've experienced first-hand the many benefits options can bring to the table in up and down markets. Today's new technology and affordable software programs make options even more attractive as they allow every investor to be armed with all the facts needed to make quick, well-calculated decisions. These programs model the behavior of options trades for you—and give you information previously accessible only to the professionals.

Once you've embraced the use of options, you must also exercise the discipline and vigilance needed to map out a game plan and stick with it. You need to establish your own trading guidelines regarding when to close positions, how much risk you are willing to take, and clearly identify what you are trying to achieve with each trade; otherwise, it will be exceedingly difficult to profit from trading options, or from trading other investment vehicles for that matter.

Many traders claim to have a plan, but it's typically just a highly limited "best-case scenario" strategy. They'll say: "I like Proctor & Gamble, so I bought 1,000 shares when it was at $75. If it goes to $150, I'll sell." Or—worse yet—they may have *no* idea when they would really be willing to sell—and no clue how high Proctor & Gamble could realistically go in the short term. Would they sell if the stock went up to just $98 or $125—or hold on and wait for a home run? Conversely, what if that stock *drops* in price? Do you hang on and, if so, for how long? Without a plan of action—and the discipline to stick to it—you're treating your investment portfolio like a lottery ticket. It's fine to invest on a whim or a hunch, then sit back and hope it all goes in the right direction. But it's infinitely better to plan for *all* eventualities, not just the positive ones. And by incorporating the appropriate option strategy into your game plan, you could generate significant gains no matter what direction the market takes.

We're all used to insuring our automobiles, right? When you're invested primarily in the equities markets without the "insurance" options afford, it's the same as driving around without any car insurance. Purchasing those 1,000 shares of Proctor & Gamble at $75 per share is like driving off the lot with a brand new $75,000 Mercedes—and with absolutely **no** insurance. You have no downside protection if your stock crashes and huge liability exposure if your portfolio gets hurt. None of us would risk our beautiful new luxury car like that—so why would you do it with your hard earned investment dollars?

Now let's say you agree with my concept of planning and managing your risk. You set levels at which you'd sell your Procter & Gamble if it goes up, and at what price you'd sell out if the trade moves against you. You enter a sell stop order, which you believe will protect you against loss beyond a certain point, since a sell stop order instructs your broker to sell your stock at the market price if the stock trades at or below the price you've set. Unfortunately, stocks often gap up or down, so your sell stop may not be executed until Procter & Gamble has traded significantly lower than where you placed your stop. It's as if you got car insurance from a stranger on the street who may not be there when you really need them.

Purchasing a put option would be a much better choice. The put gives the owner the right to sell at a specified price. The put gives the investor the confidence that he or she will not suffer catastrophic loss should a worst-case scenario play out. That confidence comes at a price, as does insurance for that Mercedes. Zero-deductible insurance is more expensive than $500-deductible insurance, and in both cases you lose the premium paid if you don't need to use the insurance at all. But when was the last time you heard someone complain, "Boy, I wish I would have crashed my Mercedes so that I didn't waste my money!"?

Insuring your investment should be just as routine as insuring your vehicle and if you take time to learn how to use basic option strategies, including the ones outlined in this book, you can drastically improve the odds that, in the future, you will be richer rather than poorer.

After several decades in the trading markets, I've experienced everything from strong robust markets, to choppy and even downright nasty ones. Throughout the changing investment climates, options have remained a key investment of choice to protect my trading dollars—to enhance my returns—and for pure speculation plays.

Over the years I've also seen the impact that computers and new software programs have had on options trading. Each new improvement on the technology side makes option trading easier, more accurate, and increases your chance for sustained success. With the benefits options offer—and the simplicity trading software provides—options remain an incredibly powerful and rewarding trading tool. I encourage every investor to explore them in more detail.

This booklet is an excellent starting point. Jim and Steve, who manage analysis and education at the highly regarded OptionVue Research, have done an excellent job making fairly complex concepts very understandable. They limit the scope to three key reasons for using options: speculation, enhancing your returns, and managing risk in your portfolio. They also emphasize the same core values I espouse, repeating the mantra of "discipline" and the need to establish trading guidelines to follow. Obviously, there are many more nuances to options trading than you'll find in this book. But it provides an excellent starting point for newcomers, and is also a great refresher course for experienced traders who have let trading habits get sloppy.

As anyone who's seen my live training workshops knows, I'm *extremely* animated—even passionate—about options trading. I love everything about the whole process, and find it both fascinating and rewarding. I hope anyone not currently including options in their investment program will consider going down that path after reading this work. I welcome all of you to join me on the journey!

Jon "Dr. J" Najarian
PTI Securities

# Chapter 1

# WHY OPTIONS?

For anyone who is uncertain about how the stock market will act in the near term—and that describes just about every stockholder—options present tremendous opportunities. They let you leverage your investment capital, give you greater flexibility when making investment decisions, and allow you to tailor your risk to fit your personal comfort level. In short, options can be used effectively for a number of different purposes, including the three primary ones we will address in this book which cover using them: (1) to speculate in the market for profit, (2) to earn income and enhance your investment returns, and (3) to protect against a temporary decline in a stock's value, or to hedge your entire portfolio against market risk.

## The Benefits of Trading with Options

A key benefit options offer over other investment vehicles is that an option trader can profit in either an up *or* a down market. When you buy an option, you are hoping that the underlying stock will move in the direction you want. If you're right, you make a profit. If you're wrong, you lose money. But it's really all a matter of two things: Time—since the option contract always expires at some point, and timing. Consistent with all forms of investing, timing is everything in options trading.

This book attempts to show how adding options to your trading arsenal can help you better reach your investment goals. How you use options depends on what you hope to achieve and how much risk you can afford to take. Some investors think of options only as a stand-alone and speculative product. And they can certainly be used that way. However, the potential uses of options go far beyond pure speculation—as we will endeavor to demonstrate throughout the book.

This work will cover a number of option strategies that illustrate how versatile options are in helping you meet your personal investment goals while also controlling your risk. If you want to protect long stock positions, discount your basis, leverage capital, or insure paper profits—an option strategy exists to help you. If you want to avoid as much risk as possible, some very conservative strategies are presented that will enable you to manage risk while also enhancing portfolio profits. Just as an experienced chess player sees the entire board and does not base strategies on the movement of a single piece, a well-informed investor is able to integrate options into a larger portfolio strategy.

## The Leverage Inherent in Options

Each option contract gives you the right to buy (a call option) or sell (a put option) 100 shares of stock at a specific price (the strike price) by a specific date in time (the expiration date). When you buy an option, you hope that the stock will move in your predicted direction, and quickly enough to make a profit. The cost of the option—the option premium—is far less than the cost of buying 100 shares of stock. For example, it would cost $6,000 to buy 100 shares of a stock currently worth $60 a share. If the option premium for a call option on this stock is $4, you could buy the option for only $400. That gives you the right to buy 100 shares of the stock—but you don't *have* to. That $400 gives you control over $6,000 worth of stock. That's leverage.

> When you buy an option, you hope that the stock will move in your predicted direction, and quickly enough to make a profit.

You get a different type of leverage when you buy a put. A put option gives you the right to *sell* 100 shares of stock, but you don't have to own the stock. The put buyer hopes the price of the stock goes down. If it does, the put becomes more valuable and can be sold for a profit.

As a pure speculation, buying calls or puts gives you the chance to make money on the movement of stocks, but without having to pay out big money at great risk. When you own shares of stock, the big risk is that the value might fall. So if you invest $6,000 in 100 shares of stock and its market value falls to $30, you then lose $3,000. But if you buy a call option for a premium of $4, the most you will ever lose is $400. So while you control the same 100 shares of stock, you have only a fraction of the capital at risk.

Of course, using options in this way also entails risk. If the stock price does not move in the direction you anticipated, the value of the option will drop. Even if the stock price doesn't move at all, time works against you. The ever-looming expiration date means that value goes out of the option day-by-day,

> While leverage is desirable, it comes with some amount of risk.

and you *can* lose the entire premium paid for the option. So even while leverage is desirable, it comes with some amount of risk.

## Playing the Downside with Options

Many stock investors think only with a bullish perspective. But as experience has shown, stock prices across the board can decline for long periods. Owning stock when this happens can be an expensive experience. However, going long the stock is not the only way to invest in the stock market. If you think a stock will go down, you can sell the stock short.

Short selling stock is a potentially high-risk venture. When you short a stock, you believe the value will fall, and if you are right, you can then close out the short position at a profit. Short sellers open the position by borrowing the stock from their broker at a reasonable interest rate and then selling it on the open market. To close the position, they buy the stock back—the opposite of the traditional buy-then-sell pattern every stockholder knows. For short sellers, the risk is that their timing is wrong, and the market value of the stock rises. When that happens—it can cause big losses, which are theoretically *unlimited.* That's a very big risk to take—and short selling may not be an appropriate strategy for most stock investors.

However, put options in place of stock to play the down market presents the same opportunity, but with less risk. When you buy puts, you make a profit if the price of the underlying stock falls. So in a bear market, put buying can be profitable—assuming the timing is right. At the same time, your risk is limited to only the premium paid.

## Managing Risk and the Various Option Strategies

With options, *you* control how much risk you have. You can buy one option or several. You're not necessarily at the mercy of a fickle market that can make or break a portfolio with devastating results. You can manage your risk by putting in only as much as you want to expose to possible loss.

The main advantage stockholders have is that they can afford to wait out the market. Even if a stock loses half its value, the stock investor can just continue collecting dividends and wait for the market to go in the opposite direction. While the option buyer may have less risk, they have less time also. While some options like LEAPS may have a year or two until expiration, most options last only a few months. If you don't make your profit before expiration, you just lose. That's why it is so critical to have some basic options education—to familiarize yourself with all the various strategies available.

> With options, *you* control how much risk you have.

One of the great things about options is their versatility. There is a wide range of strategies available, and each of these strategies has a different risk/reward profile. Some strategies are high-risk, like the speculative buying of call and put options; others are designed to profit if specific future expectations are met. People who are unfamiliar with options typically view them as high risk, speculative investments, and overlook more conservative benefits many options strategies offer for (1) protecting portfolio positions, (2) spreading and hedging risk, and (3) generating additional income on your stock holdings. These three strategies make options one of the more interesting and practical ways to invest, and they are especially useful when dealing with the challenges of volatile market conditions. In the following chapters, we will focus on specific option strategies available that can be applied to help you protect your positions and/or your portfolio, hedge risk and enhance your overall returns.

## Profiting with Options in Other Situations

One of the significant advantages of options is their flexibility. When you own stock, you make a profit only if one thing happens: the stock's price moves *above* its current trading range. But options are so flexible that you can even make a profit if a stock stays within a limited trading range. Calendar spreads and short straddles are some of the strategies designed to produce profits if the stock price *doesn't* move. This means an option position can be profitable even if the stock shows very little movement in the period of time you have the position open.

Other strategies are designed to create profits if the stock price moves in *either* direction, such as long straddles. In this case, you don't really care what direction the stock price moves, as long as it *does* move. Because options can be used in so many combinations, their applications are very deep and rich. Once you understand how to use time as the key element in creating option profits, you will be well on your way to developing winning strategies that work specifically for you.

## Using Options for Insurance

Options can also be used to "insure" your position. For example, if you buy one put option for every 100 shares of stock you own, it gives you downside protection. As the stock price drops, the put goes up in value. And no matter how far the stock price drops, you have the right to sell your stock at the strike price specified by the put option.

You can also insure a short stock position. If you have sold stock short, the worst outcome would be a rising stock price. You can insure against that by buying one call option for every 100 shares you have sold short. As the stock price rises, the call goes up in value. And again, no matter how much the stock price rises, you have the right to buy the stock at the strike price specified by the call option.

You can use options to insure your portfolio as a whole. There are options available on many different stock indexes, including the Dow

Jones Industrial Average, the S&P 500, and the NASDAQ 100. Buying puts on the index that is closest to the composition of your portfolio gives you protection from market risk. When the overall market drops, it is likely that most of the stocks in your portfolio will also drop in price. But the index puts will gain in value, offsetting much, if not all, of the drop in value of your stocks.

## The Adventure Begins

The United States stock markets represent one of the largest concentrations of wealth in the world. And anyone with a little capital can potentially make profits from it. What does it take to succeed? Top traders and investors all say that discipline is the key to success, because without it you will let a losing trade become a portfolio killer.

> Knowledge and education are essential ingredients for option trading success.

Knowledge and education are essential ingredients for option trading success, but your efforts will definitely be in vain if you don't have the discipline to follow a trading plan. Trading presents years of frustrating challenges for some, and a lifetime of financial rewards for others. Hopefully, this book will help you enter the latter group, as you learn to embrace options and incorporate them into your ongoing investment program.

# *Chapter 2*

# USING CALL OPTIONS FOR SPECULATION AND INCOME

U nderstanding the terminology and rules for options is necessary before you start trading them. Beyond that, you need to develop a thorough understanding of risk and how it varies from one strategy to another. Remember that options can be used in a wide variety of strategies, from conservative to very high-risk. Many traders are first attracted to options for high-leverage directional trading. Directional trading is when a trader believes he knows which way a stock price will move and opens an option position to take advantage of it.

> Understanding the terminology and rules for options is necessary before you start trading them.

With stock you only have to worry about one thing—price. In the landscape of options you have three shifting parameters: the price of the underlying stock, daily time decay, and volatility. Changes in any one of these will affect the value of your options. We have already mentioned how the value of calls and puts are affected by changes in the underlying stock price. Time is another concept that is fairly easy to understand. The fact that options will expire and may become worthless in the future is an important and key feature in every option strategy; ultimately, it can determine whether your option trading decisions are profitable or not.

The effect volatility has on an options value is usually harder for beginners to understand. Ideally, what traders would like to know is what future volatility will be. But since we don't know that, we try to guess what it will be. The beginning point for this guess is statistical (sometimes called historical) volatility, or SV. The SV tells us what the actual volatility has been for this stock over a given period of time. However there is another measure of volatility called implied volatility, or IV, which traders use to decide if options are cheap or expensive.

There are different models for pricing options, but most will yield a price relatively close to each other. When you put in all the variables (stock price, time, interest rates, dividends, and volatility), you get an answer that tells you, based on those numbers, what an option *should* be worth. But what if you work the model backwards? After all, you know what the option *is* trading at. You can also find out the other variables (stock price, interest rates, dividends, and time left in the option) with a bit of research. In fact, the only thing you *don't* know for sure is what future volatility will be.

When you put all those numbers in and work the pricing model backwards you get implied volatility, so named because it is the volatility *implied* by the actual option price. So IV is calculated based on the currently traded option premiums. Option traders often say that "Premium levels are high" or "Premium levels are low." What they really mean is that current IV is high or low. Once you understand this concept, then it makes sense that you should try to buy options when their premiums are cheap, and sell options when they are expensive.

> Your approach to trading options should always be based on the level of risk you think is appropriate.

Your approach to trading options should always be based on the level of risk you think is appropriate. Most investors use options as part of a larger strategy based on selection of stocks. Thus, a study of fundamental and technical indicators is the logical starting point. Next we explain some basic option trading strategies using calls. We will explore the use of calls to speculate on the direction of a stock using both a simple call purchase and debit spreads. Then we will look at how you can use calls to generate additional income using covered call writes and credit spreads. We will talk a little about the special case of LEAPS, and how they can be used as a substitute for stock. Our goal here is to demonstrate how to increase your investing profits without exposing yourself to unacceptable risks.

## The Long Call Strategy—Using Calls for Speculation

Most investors start by buying stock, and they are used to thinking in terms of purchasing a stock for its potential to go up in price. So new option traders usually start out simply buying call options because it seems similar to what they are used to doing. When a call option on stock is purchased (also called "going long the option"), the call holder is able to control the stock without actually possessing it, and does so for a fraction of the cost. Buying calls has been one of the most popular strategies with investors since listed options were first introduced. Before moving onto more complicated strategies, an investor should thoroughly understand buying and holding call options.

A long call is a leveraged alternative to the stock itself. As the stock price increases, the option value increases by more (sometimes much more) on a percentage basis. This leverage can result in large percentage profits, because purchasing calls requires a lower up-front capital commitment than an outright purchase of the stock. In fact your profits are theoretically unlimited, since there is no limit on how high a stock price can go. This strategy also has limited risk, since you cannot lose more than you paid for the option. However, while the potential loss is limited in terms of dollars, you can lose 100% of the premium paid for the call. The performance graph on page 20 shows the (limited) risk and unlimited potential profit for the long call strategy.

The three lines in the previous figure graphically illustrate how time decay affects this position. The **dotted** line represents the long call's theoretical performance as of today, the **solid** line represents the performance at expiration (the final day of trading), and the dashed line represents the performance of this option halfway between today and expiration. Notice also that the intersection of each line with the $0 profit line represents that time frame's break-even point; and this break-even point moves farther to the right as time passes.

The question now becomes: which option should I buy? Every stock that trades options has at least four different expiration months with

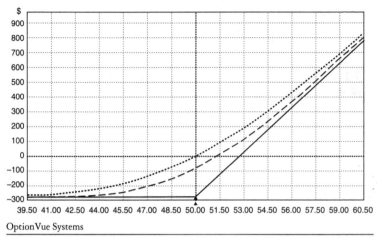

$

900 ........
800 ........
700 ........
600 ........
500 ........
400 ........
300 ........
200 ........
100 ........
0 ........
−100 ........
−200 ........
−300 ........

39.50 41.00 42.50 44.00 45.50 47.00 48.50 50.00 51.50 53.00 54.50 56.00 57.50 59.00 60.50

OptionVue Systems

Profit/Loss by Change in XYZ Common Price

many different strike prices available. Depending on the strike price and time left until expiration, options respond in very different ways to price movements in the stock.

Calls with strike prices higher than the current stock price are called *out-of the-money* options; if the expiration date were today, they would be worthless. Out-of-the-money options have value only because there is still time left for the stock price to move above the strike price. The part of an option's price attributable to time is called time value or *time premium*.

An *at-the-money* call option is one whose strike price is equal to (or in practice, very close to) the stock price. Again, the premium paid for an at-the-money option is entirely due to time. Of course, it won't take much of an increase in the stock price to turn this into an in-the-money option.

An *in-the-money* call option has a strike price that is lower than the current stock price. The difference between the strike price and current stock price, called its *intrinsic value,* is the amount the option is in the money. But as long as there is still time left until the expiration day, an in-the-money option will also have some time value as well. That means the price of an option can be broken down into two parts: intrinsic value and time value. Next is a diagram showing how an option's price is broken down between intrinsic value and time premium, depending on whether it is at, in, or out-of-the-money.

| Stock Price at $50 | | | | |
| --- | --- | --- | --- | --- |
| Call Strike | Option Price ($) | Time Value ($) | Intrinsic Value ($) | ATM, OTM, or ITM |
| 60.00 | 0.50 | 0.50 | 0.00 | Out-of-the-money |
| 55.00 | 2.00 | 2.00 | 0.00 | Out-of-the-money |
| 50.00 | 4.00 | 4.00 | 0.00 | At-the-money |
| 45.00 | 7.00 | 2.00 | 5.00 | In-the-money |
| 40.00 | 10.50 | 0.50 | 10.00 | In-the-money |

The farther out of the money an option is, the cheaper it will be, and the higher the leverage. So if the stock makes a quick move in your favor, an out-of-the-money option will do the best job of multiplying your money. However, if this move does not happen quickly, the out-of-the-money option's performance is likely to disappoint you. At-the-money and in-the-money options move more like the underlying stock because their *delta* is greater. The delta of an at-the-money option is typically around .50—meaning that a one-point move in the stock translates into a half point move for the option. In-the-money options have deltas approaching 1 and they move almost point-for-point with the stock. Often the best balance of factors can be found using at-the-money, or just in-the-money, options.

There are several reasons to buy options. Those who would like to participate in movement of the stock price but lack the resources to buy it outright can buy an option for a fraction of the cost. The limited risk appeals to some investors that want to limit their downside to just the price of the option. Finally, there are the people who trade options to take advantage of the leverage available when speculating on price movements.

> There are several reasons to buy options.

## The Bull Call Spread—An Alternative to the Long Call Strategy

We mentioned that beginning option traders tend to start out buying calls. They should really consider the benefits of spreads. The bull call spread is used when you anticipate that the price of a particular stock will increase but want less risk than you get with a call purchase. It involves simultaneously buying a call option, while selling another call option at a higher strike price in the same expiration month. The biggest advantage of the bull call spread is that it lessens the effects of the two biggest enemies of long options—time and volatility. It is less sensitive to the day-to-day fluctuations in the stock price, so it is a more relaxed style of trading. The other benefit of a bull call spread versus the long call is that you risk less capital for an equal number of contracts. That reduces your break-even point, and increases the probability of making a profit.

In a bull call spread, you buy calls at one strike price and sell others at a higher strike price. The calls you sell discount the purchase price of the calls you buy. For example, let's say a stock currently trading at $90 offers calls at the 100 and 110 strikes. The 100 calls cost $6 and the $110s are worth $4. So buying one of the 100 calls would cost you $600. But with the bull call spread, you could buy the 100 calls for $600 and sell the 110s for $400, which will cost you the net difference of $200. So for the price of a single call option, you could afford to buy three of the bull call spreads. So what is the full risk and profit potential of the bull call spread?

Worst case: If the stock price does not rise above $100 before expiration, you will be out $200 per spread for the whole transaction (plus trading costs).

Best case: If the stock price hits or exceeds $110 per share by expiration day, you will profit. Your gain will be the difference between the strikes ($10) minus the cost of the spread ($2) times the 100 shares, for a total profit of $800 for each spread you purchased.

The full range of possibilities for this strategy is illustrated in the figure on page 23.

In the example above, you would have to spend $600 for each call at the strike price of 100, and all of that is time value. But the bull call spread only cost you $200. Putting $600 into a call that is all time value is a very high-risk strategy. With the spread, selling the call at a higher strike price offset much of the cost, and the risk is considerably lower. In times of exceptional volatility, options are more expensive. That puts

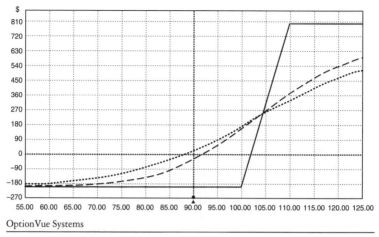

$

810
720
630
540
450
360
270
180
90
0
−90
−180
−270

55.00 60.00 65.00 70.00 75.00 80.00 85.00 90.00 95.00 100.00 105.00 110.00 115.00 120.00 125.00

OptionVue Systems

Profit/Loss by Change in COMPANY A Common Price

the option buyer at a disadvantage. However, the option spreader gets to neutralize much of this effect by selling an overpriced option at the same time that he buys an overpriced option.

## The Covered Call—Generating Additional Income from Your Stock Portfolio

Covered writing is often touted as a safe way to generate extra income from a stock portfolio. It follows naturally from the simple purchase of stock, is relatively easy to explain, and results in immediate income. And it seems to be just as safe as simply investing in stock. While speculative call buyers usually hold their position for a relatively short period of time, the covered call writer often expects to hold his position to expiration. The best part is that covered writers make money during periods when their stock holdings go nowhere. The income generated can be impressive, with annual returns of 30% or more. Remember though, such returns are possible only if the stock goes up or remains at around the same price.

There are two ways to sell calls, "naked" or "covered." A naked call exists when a sold call has no hedge or any position that mitigates or removes the risk. Owning 100 shares of the stock for every sold call option hedges the short position and removes some of the risk. The hedge could also be a long call at a different strike price, like in the bull call spread strategy discussed previously.

Remember also that an option is a contract, with different rights and obligations for buyers and sellers. When you buy a call option, it means you have the right to buy 100 shares at the strike price specified. When you *sell* calls, the owner of that call option can impose the right on you. If the option buyer chooses to exercise his rights, you as the seller have the *obligation* to deliver the specified number of shares at the specified (strike) price. The danger of the naked call strategy is that the stock price might rise above the strike price of the call option you sold. In that case, you would be required to deliver 100 shares at the fixed strike price, which could be considerably lower than current market value of the stock. Therefore, the risk of writing uncovered calls is unacceptable for the majority of investors.

> An option is a contract, with different rights and obligations for buyers and sellers.

So you need to hedge a sold option in order to avoid that risk. When you own 100 shares of stock and you sell a call on that stock, the strategy is no longer high-risk. In the event of exercise, you own the 100 shares and can simply deliver them to satisfy the contractual demands of the exercised call. A covered call writer is primarily seeking income. They also receive some downside protection (by the amount of the premium received), but the tradeoff is that the maximum possible profit is limited by the sold call. But this can be a worthwhile strategy as long as you pick your strike price carefully. For example, let's say you originally bought 100 shares of stock at $36 per share. You sell a 40 call and receive a premium of $2. Because you get $200 for selling the call, your basis in the stock is discounted down to $34 per share:

| | |
|---|---|
| Original purchase price | $3,600 |
| Less: call premium | −200 |
| Adjusted basis in stock | $3,400 |

In this situation, you will profit in the event of exercise, but your maximum profit is $6 a share (you receive $4,000 no matter how high the stock price at the time of exercise). If the stock price falls below $34, you would have a net loss. The range of profit and loss is illustrated in the figure below:

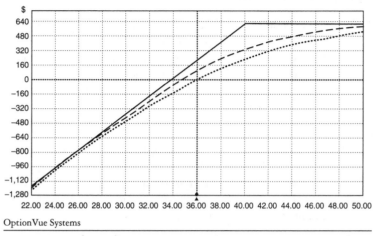

OptionVue Systems

Profit/Loss by Change in COMPANY B Common Price

If the stock price is higher than $40 per share by expiration, the position is in the "fixed profit range," and you will net $600 on the transaction:

| | |
|---|---|
| Strike price × 100 shares | $4,000 |
| Discounted basis in stock | −3,400 |
| Fixed profit upon exercise | $ 600 |

The range below the discounted price level is the "loss range." You lose $1 per share for each point the stock falls below $32 per share, just as you would if you simply owned the stock. But remember, the stock was originally purchased at $34 per share.

It is the middle range in this example that highlights the advantage of selling covered calls. As long as the stock remains between $34 and $40 per share, you are better off selling the call. The short call will expire worthless, or you can close it out with a closing purchase transaction. Once the call expires or is bought to close, you can then repeat the process by selling another call. This sequence can be repeated as often as you wish.

Covered call writers have a distinct advantage over writers of naked calls because exercise is not catastrophic. It simply means you keep the option premium, and sell your 100 shares of stock at a profit as well. You also continue to receive dividends as long as you own the stock. There are three possible outcomes to the covered call write:

1. **You close the position.** You can always cancel out a short position by a closing purchase transaction. In this case you begin with an opening sale; if the call option later declines in value, you can purchase it back and close the position. The difference between the "sale" and "buy" prices is profit, and reported as a short-term capital gain in the year the position is closed.

2. **The option expires worthless.** There is always the chance that a short out-of-the-money call position will never gain in-the-money value. As expiration nears, its time value begins to disappear quickly. At expiration, it becomes worthless. In that case, the entire premium is profit, and is reported as a short-term capital gain in the year the option expired.

3. **The option is exercised.** The third outcome is exercise. If the buyer were to exercise, your 100 shares would be called away at the strike price and you would keep the collected premium. This happens only if the stock price is higher than the strike price, thus making it an in-the-money option. Exercise can take place at any time, so if you sell a call you have to be prepared for this possibility.

As a general rule of thumb, it makes sense to sell covered calls only if you are completely willing to have your 100 shares called away. However, if the stock's value rises and is close to the covered call's strike price, you might want to avoid exercise. You can do this by exchanging one call for another in an exchange called "rolling up." For example, you could close out the short call with a purchase transaction, and then sell another call option in a farther month with a higher strike price. You can roll up and out indefinitely as the stock price continues to rise as long as you are willing to continue using your 100 shares to cover the short call position.

> You can always cancel out a short position by a closing purchase transaction.

Time is the friend of the option seller. While time decay is a big problem for option buyers, it is the key to success for option sellers. The more the option value falls, the more you profit. The real beauty of selling covered options is

not only that you can generate income with little additional risk, but the fact that you can repeat the process over and over. As each option position is closed or expires worthless, you can sell another call against the same 100 shares—and repeat that as many times as you like. So your 100 shares can produce profits not just from price appreciation and dividends, but also from call premium.

But there is some downside to the covered call strategy. First if the stock quickly goes up, even doubles or triples in price, your profit is limited. But of course you bought the stock in the first place expecting it to increase in value. And you were right! Unfortunately, in this case you will profit very little from it because your gains are limited by the call sold.

What if there is a significant drop in the stock price? Your calls really do very little to protect you against losses as the market falls. You get to keep the premium from selling the call (when it expires worthless), but you still own stock that is now worth much less than you paid for it.

Not everyone should sell calls, particularly those that expect very rapid stock price appreciation. Even though it is a profitable strategy, it works best as part of a broader investment program. Understand exactly what possible outcomes could occur and be willing to closely monitor your positions so you can react if you need to. For those who do understand the covered call, it is a conservative strategy that can enhance investment returns significantly.

# Long-Term Speculation—The Special Case of LEAPS

LEAPS—Long Term Equity AnticiPation Securities—are options that have a far longer life than standard options, with a time frame of years rather than months. Only about 10% of optionable stocks have LEAPS, primarily the most popular high-volume stocks. LEAPS have significant time premium and are more expensive than standard options, but still cheaper than purchasing 100 shares of the stock. In many ways, you can think of them as a substitute for buying the stock.

The primary use of LEAPS is for speculation. As implied by their name, you might purchase a call LEAPS if you anticipate long-term appreciation in the stock price, or a put LEAPS if you think that the stock price is likely to decline over a long period of time. While the risk graph for a long call LEAPS position looks exactly like the long call shown earlier, the longer time period adds some additional risk. In particular, the large time premium associated with LEAPS means they are especially sensitive to changes in implied volatility. There's no worse feeling than seeing the market move in the anticipated direction, but your options gaining very little. Historical volatility charts are available from the best option-oriented Web sites and software companies such as Option-Vue Systems International, and these charts can help you determine if a stock's options are cheap or expensive on a historical basis.

> LEAPS provide great flexibility because of their higher time value.

LEAPS can also be used as a substitute for stock in strategies such as the covered call just discussed. In that strategy, you would buy the longer-term LEAPS option and sell a shorter-term option on the same stock. The short option is covered, or hedged, with the long LEAPS option. Technically, this is really a horizontal, or calendar, spread. But many of the same techniques from the covered call strategy can be applied here, including the rolling of the short option as it is closed or expires worthless. And given the variations in time value, you can also profit from simply playing the timing of the spread. We will discuss the horizontal spread later in this book, and you should be familiar with the associated risks before trying it. The point, however, is that LEAPS provide great flexibility because of their higher time value.

# The Bear Call Spread—Collecting Income from Option Selling

The bear call spread is a limited-risk strategy that essentially profits from the decay of time value. In one respect, it is the exact opposite of the bull call spread; you are hoping for a decline in the stock. You buy a bull call spread hoping its value will increase, not unlike a stock. But with the bear call spread, you receive a credit to your account when you place the trade, and your goal is to keep it. The credit received is your potential profit. You can never make more than that. You can lose it, however, and more if the stock moves up. You can even make money with a bear call spread if the stock price doesn't move at all between now and expiration. You just don't want it to move up.

To construct a bear call spread, you sell a call option at a lower strike price, and offset that by buying a call option at a higher strike price farther out-of-the-money. For example, let's say a $48 stock you think will fall in value has 50 and 55 call options available, with the 50 calls valued at $5, and the 55 calls valued at $3. Because the 50 calls will be closer to the current stock price, you will receive a net premium (or credit to your account) for this type of trade.

> Your potential profits and losses are limited in the bear call spread.

If the stock does fall in value, the 50 calls you sold will also decline in value. They can then be closed at a profit, or allowed to expire worthless. The only reason to buy the calls at the higher strike price calls is to reduce your risk (and the possible loss) in case you are wrong and the stock goes up. That means your maximum risk exposure is equal to the difference between the strikes, minus the premium received when the bear call spread was opened.

In the above example, you would be paid $200 for every 50–55 spread you opened, minus transaction fees. So your maximum risk exposure is going to be $300. If the stock were to rise, you could close out the position and take a net loss. The worst case scenario is if the short 50 call was exercised before you could close the position. Then you would be required to deliver 100 shares at $50. With the bear call spread, you can always exercise your 55 call to satisfy that requirement, losing a net of $300 on the transaction.

The bear call spread in this example would be profitable as long as the stock finishes at or below $52 per share by the expiration date. Your potential profits and losses are limited in the bear call spread, and even in the best case your profit will never be more than the initial credit received. The possible outcomes for this trade are shown in following figure.

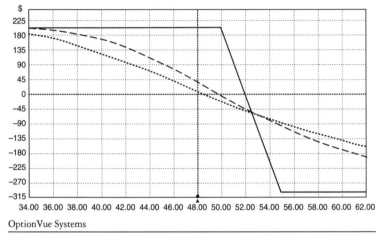

OptionVue Systems

Profit/Loss by Change in COMPANY C Common Price

In contrast to the bull call spread, where you simply pay the difference between the premiums of the two options, a credit spread involves a *margin requirement* based on the difference in the strike prices. You would be required to put up the difference between the strike prices (in this example 5, or $500 per spread) minus the credit you received ($200 in this case). This means it will cost you only $300 to place this trade.

> The options trader must always be ready for the unexpected.

Remember, every option strategy that looks good on paper will work *only* if the underlying stock behaves in a particular way. You can design strategies that will be profitable if the stock moves in a specific direction; if the stock trades within a desired range; or if movement occurs within the time limits imposed on all the options. But the options trader must always be ready for the unexpected. The unpredictability of the market characterizes stocks and, to an even greater degree, it defines the risk in options.

# A Word on Risk Management

With all option strategies, you should know the potential loss as well as the potential gain before you enter a trade, and be willing to accept the loss if it does occur. Experienced traders who are successful year in and year out will attest that risk management is the key to long term profitability, particularly limiting the potential loss for each trade to a certain percentage level of your trading account. In interviews with some of these individuals, the figure most often cited is 5%, meaning that no trade should cost more than 5% of your trading account. A figure higher than this increases the odds that emotion will cloud your judgment. Your trading activity could then take on a character closer to gambling. Bottom Line: Manage risk wisely by limiting the potential loss from each trade to 5% of your trading account.

# Chapter 3

# USING PUTS FOR SPECULATION, INCOME, AND PROTECTION

Americans are optimists; we think that everything is going to look better tomorrow, including stock prices. So we naturally tend to favor call options, because when the stock price goes up we will make a nice profit. In fact, when exchange traded options were introduced in 1973 there were no put options available, only calls! Put options on stocks didn't begin trading until four years later, in June 1977. The fact is, however, that the various stock markets (and the individual stocks they are comprised of) do not always go up, but can have long seasons of bearish activity. Buying put options allows you to profit when this happens.

> Americans are optimists; we think that everything is going to look better tomorrow, including stock prices.

In the previous chapter, we demonstrated a variety of potential uses for call options with an emphasis on speculation and income. In this chapter, we explain how to use two strategies—the long put and the bear put spread—when speculating on an expected drop in price. We will also look at opportunities to generate income by selling naked puts and credit (bull put) spreads when you expect a stock price to increase. Finally, we will examine how to use puts options to protect your stockholdings. The nature of puts makes them an ideal tool for hedging risk when you are concerned about downward price moves in volatile markets.

# The Long Put Strategy—Betting on the Downside

When you buy a put, you acquire the right to *sell* 100 shares of stock. Like the call option, the put option is a contract that specifies the price (the strike price) you have the right to sell the stock at, and by what date (the expiration date). The put option buyer has the *right* to sell the stock at the strike price, but he doesn't have to. The put option seller, on the other hand, has the *obligation* to buy the stock at the strike price if the put is assigned. Most investors find it easier to understand calls, but the put gives the investor many advantages not available with calls. So the time spent learning about puts and how to use them properly is time well spent.

> Time spent learning about puts and how to use them properly is time well spent.

Many of the option terms used are the opposite depending on whether they are used with calls or puts. When talking about put options, in-the-money refers to a put whose strike price is *higher* than the current stock price. At-the money still describes an option whose strike price and stock price are the same, but an out-of-the-money put has a strike price that is *lower* than the current stock price. Just as in call options, the out-of-the-money put option position has higher leverage and more risk compared to an at-the-money or in-the-money option.

| Stock Price at $50 | | | | |
| --- | --- | --- | --- | --- |
| Put Strike | Option Price ($) | Time Value ($) | Intrinsic Value ($) | ATM, OTM, or ITM |
| 60.00 | 10.50 | 0.50 | 10.00 | In-the-money |
| 55.00 | 7.00 | 2.00 | 5.00 | In-the-money |
| 50.00 | 4.00 | 4.00 | 0.00 | At-the-money |
| 45.00 | 2.00 | 2.00 | 0.00 | Out-of-the-money |
| 40.00 | 0.50 | 0.50 | 0.00 | Out-of-the-money |

As we saw earlier, an option buyer can only lose the amount paid for the option; nothing more. With the call option the profit potential was theoretically unlimited, since there is no limit on how high a stock price can go. But with a put option there *is* a limit, since the price of a stock can never go lower than zero. Still, that leaves lots of room to make a profit with most stocks. The same qualities of leverage, limited risk, and large potential profits that make buying calls attractive apply to put options as well. Just remember, the option buyer's enemy is time decay. As each day goes by the option loses some of its value, so speculative put buying works best when you are working in a shorter time frame.

The performance graph next for a long put position clearly illustrates the limited risk and big profit potential for this strategy:

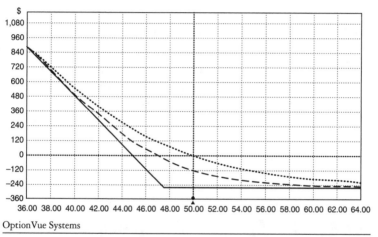

OptionVue Systems

Profit/Loss by Change in XYZ Common Price

Again, the three lines illustrate how time decay affects the position with the **solid** line representing the possible outcomes on expiration day. The **dashed** line represents the theoretical performance of this option halfway between today and expiration, while the **dotted** line shows what should happen if the stock price were to move to the appropriate price today.

As with call options, there are many different strike prices and expiration dates available for put options. Since options with different strikes and durations respond differently to price movements in the stock, the decision about which option to buy is also important with puts. In no way should a cheaper price influence your decision about which option to purchase. Remember, the cheaper option would be out-of-the-money (below the stock price), and buying them has a lower probability of success than buying at- or in-the-money options.

Also, remember that the time remaining before the expiration date is a key factor in the decision criteria. Time is working against the option buyer as soon as the order is executed. Decide how long you think it will take for the stock to make the expected price move. Now double it. That should give you a reasonable idea of what expiration month to consider.

> **Time is working against the option buyer as soon as the order is executed.**

Finally, always know the current volatility situation by looking at a volatility chart (discussed in more detail in the next chapter). This allows you to know whether the options are historically cheap or expensive for that stock. If implied volatility is very high, you may want to consider buying deeper-in-the-money options. These options have less time premium, so they are not as sensitive to changes in volatility. You may also want to consider using a spread to reduce your volatility risk in that situation. The bear put spread, which is the subject of the next section, is a good alternative to straight put buying when speculating on a drop in price. While the potential rewards from buying puts as a stand-alone strategy are high, never forget that the associated risk is very high as well.

## The Bear Put Spread—Speculating to the Downside with Spreads

Another way to play a down market is to use a bear put spread. The relative risks of an option purchase versus a vertical debit spread holds just as true with puts as when using calls. Those with bearish price expectations can buy a vertical debit spread with puts, called a bear put spread. The bear put spread fixes the maximum loss *and* possible profit. As long as the possible profit is greater than the possible loss, you would consider the risk to be worthwhile.

A bear put spread involves buying a put option, and then selling a put option located farther out-of-the-money. The risk graph of this strategy is a mirror image of the vertical debit spread using calls:

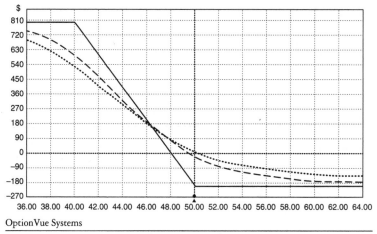

$

| | |
|---|---|
| 810 | |
| 720 | |
| 630 | |
| 540 | |
| 450 | |
| 360 | |
| 270 | |
| 180 | |
| 90 | |
| 0 | |
| −90 | |
| −180 | |
| −270 | |

36.00 38.00 40.00 42.00 44.00 46.00 48.00 50.00 52.00 54.00 56.00 58.00 60.00 62.00 64.00

OptionVue Systems

Profit/Loss by Change in COMPANY D Common Price

In this example the stock is selling right now for $50 per share. To execute this bear put spread, you buy the 50 put and sell the 40 put. If you buy the 50 put for $3, and sell the 40 put for $1, your net cost is $200 (plus trading fees). This $200 cost represents the most you can lose on this strategy; however, your maximum profit is $800—the 10-point spread minus your $200 cost.

So even if the stock were far above $50 on expiration day, the most you could lose is $200. If the stock ends up at $48 on expiration day, you will be at your breakeven point (considering the 50 strike price and two point cost of the transaction). Here you neither make nor lose any money. For every dollar below $48, you gain one point in the spread until the $40 per share level. From that price down, your profit is fixed at $800. That is a four-to-one profit advantage.

The bear put spread has the advantage of fixing the maximum loss, but has the offsetting disadvantage of fixing the maximum profit. The same characteristics of higher commissions and slower development of profit relative to an option purchase applies to the bear put spread. With this in mind, it may not appeal to everyone, but beginning option investors are usually more comfortable with the risk profile of this trade and in return accept the limitations.

# Generating Income—Selling Naked Puts

One way to generate income with puts is to simply sell them outright. While earlier we said that selling naked calls was a high risk strategy that is inappropriate for most investors, selling naked puts does not carry the same type of risk. With the short put strategy, at-the-money or just out-of-the-money puts are typically sold on stocks the investor wouldn't mind owning. If the stock stays around the current price, or advances, the investor keeps the premium when the option expires worthless.

> One way to generate income with puts is to simply sell them outright.

This strategy requires margin, so you have to put up enough cash in your brokerage account to "cover" the position in the event of exercise; thus, this strategy is also called the cash-secured put. What if the stock declines in price? In that case, the investor eventually gets assigned the shares, and the cost basis for his shares is the strike price of the put minus the premium received. That's why naked put writers should be prepared to buy the stock (and make sure they have enough funds available) before entering the position.

For example, a stock is currently trading at $42.50. An out-of-the-money put with a strike price of 40 can be sold for $2.50, resulting in a credit to your account of $250. The $250 is yours to keep, no matter what. Worse case, you'll end up paying $4,000 for 100 shares of stock. Subtract the $250, and your effective basis is $3,750, or $37.50 per share. Not a bad deal!

When you go naked with a put, you are hoping that the stock price will rise. It is a bullish position, and you have the same price expectations as you would when you buy calls. The difference, however, is that call buyers have to deal with time decay. They need the stock price to go up enough to cover the time value *and* produce a profit. Put sellers have time decay on their side, and are counting on time value to fall. A short put position can be profitable even if the stock does not move at all. So a key distinction between long calls and short puts is that it is more difficult to profit consistently from buying calls; it is relatively easy to profit consistently from selling puts. The reason: time value.

The decline in time value works against the buyer, but it is a valuable benefit to the seller.

Once you go naked on a put, you are exposed to the risk of having to buy 100 shares at the strike price. The owner of the put will only exercise it if it is in-the-money, which means you would buy the stock at a price above the current market value. That might not be a terrible outcome, as long as you consider the strike price a fair price for the stock. The market is full of inaccuracies, and there are often companies whose stock is under-valued. In those cases, having 100 shares put to you could still be a bargain, as long as you are willing to wait out the market.

> The market is full of inaccuracies, and there are often companies whose stock is under-valued.

When you sell a put, you receive a premium which is credited to your account. That is income, but it also discounts the price of the stock in the event of exercise. So if the strike price is $40, and you get a premium of $2.50 when you sell the put, your cost basis would be $37.50 per share. The range of outcomes is summarized in the figure below. Note that the risk graph is exactly the same shape as the covered call strategy, but that the short put requires less capital:

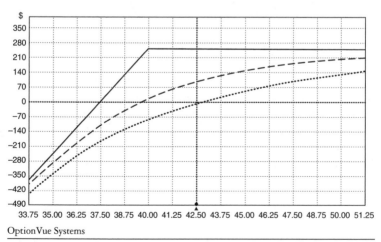

OptionVue Systems

Profit/Loss by Change in COMPANY E Common Price

If the stock exceeds the breakeven point of $37.50 (the strike price of 50 less the 2.5 points of premium), the naked put is profitable. For each dollar the stock falls below that level, you lose another point. Even so, there are steps you can take to offset these losses. For example, you could immediately sell a call against the 100 shares to produce income. You can sell naked puts and wait for them to expire; or if they quickly lose their value because the stock price goes up, you can close out the position—and then repeat the process over and over, taking your profits without risking the capital needed to buy 100 shares of stock. Naturally your brokerage firm would require funds as collateral in the event of exercise.

Your opinion about a company's true value might influence your decision to take on the risk of the naked put. When you go naked on a call, your risk is potentially unlimited, because a stock can go up without limits; but when you sell a put, your risk is limited to the difference between the striking price and zero. In theory, as long as the company has assets greater than its liabilities, your "real" risk could be considered limited to the difference between the strike price and the company's tangible book value.

## The Bull Put Spread—Collecting Income in a Bullish Environment

The bull put spread, like the bear call spread we examined earlier, is a useful tool for producing income. A bull put spread is a credit spread created by selling a put and then purchasing a put with the same expiration date at a lower strike price, farther out-of-the-money, on the same stock. This strategy is best implemented in a moderately bullish market to provide high leverage over a limited range of stock prices. While the profit on this strategy can increase by as much as 1 point for each 1 point increase in the price of the underlying, the total investment is far less than that required to buy the stock. This strategy has both limited profit potential and limited downside risk, as illustrated by the risk graph shown on page 41.

You would enter a bull put spread only if you feel confident the stock price will end at or above the strike price of the short put. You want to derive income from that opinion, and are willing to take a limited risk that you may be incorrect.

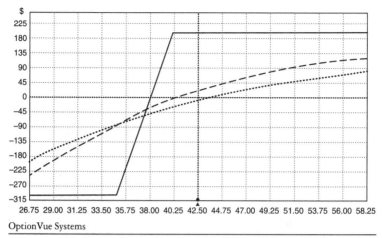

OptionVue Systems

Profit/Loss by Change in COMPANY E Common Price

A big advantage of the credit spread over selling naked puts is the lower margin requirement. With the bull put spread, you only need to put up the difference in strike prices, less the credit received. For example, to create a bull put spread on a stock currently trading at $42.50, you could sell a 40 put for $7.00, and buy the 35 put for $5.00. You would need to maintain $500 in your account to cover the risk of this position. But the net $2 premium is credited to your account, so it only costs you $300 to do the trade. By comparison, you would need to put up roughly $4,000 (or even more, depending on your broker's requirements) to sell a naked put at the 40 strike price. That's a big difference!

To exit a bull call spread, you need to sell the higher strike put and buy back the lower strike put. Of course, if things go your way you can simply let the options expire. In that case, you keep the full premium received. The maximum profit for the bull call spread occurs when the price of the underlying stock is above the strike price of the short put. If the stock price falls below that, and the option holder exercises the short put, you can exercise your long put to cover the assignment. In that case your loss is limited to the difference in strike prices, less the premium you received.

Debit and credit spreads formed using puts have performance curves that mirror those of call debit and credit spreads. The following list is a summary of the spreads we have seen so far:

| | |
|---|---|
| Call debit spread | Bullish |
| Call credit spread | Bearish |
| Put debit spread | Bearish |
| Put credit spread | Bullish |

There is little difference between the way debit spreads and credit spreads perform. Debit and credit spreads are directional trades with limited profit and limited loss. A credit spread can usually lose more than it can earn. Out-of-the-money credit spreads have the added advantage of being able to earn a profit as long as the market doesn't move too much in the opposite direction. The possible profit is equal to the credit received when you place the trade, while the maximum loss is equal the difference between the strikes minus the credit received. A logical exit strategy would be to close debit and credit spreads when they either lose or earn a fixed amount, set in advance, that you feel is acceptable.

> There is little difference between the way debit spreads and credit spreads perform.

## Using Long Puts to Protect Your Stockholdings

If you hold stock in your portfolio, you naturally worry about the possibility that their value might fall. The potential volatility of the equity markets can be of great concern to investors. When discussing the covered call strategy, we mentioned that selling calls affords a small amount of downside protection (by the amount of the premium received). But buying a put to hedge the risk of owning stock, often called a protective put, gives the investor complete protection from a drop in the stock price below the strike price of the put. This strategy is actually more conservative than the simple purchase of stock. As long as a put is held against a stock position, there is limited risk. You know at what price the stock can be sold. The only disadvantages are (1) that money will not be made until the stock moves above the combined cost of the stock and the put and (2) that the put has a finite life. But once the stock price rises above the total cost of the position, an investor has the potential for unlimited profit.

Buying a protective put involves the purchase of one put contract for every 100 shares of stock already owned or purchased. Purchasing a put against stock is similar to purchasing insurance in that the investor pays a premium (the cost of the put) to insure against a loss in the stock position. No matter what happens to the price of the stock, the put owner has the right to sell it at the strike price of the put any time prior to expiration. The risk graph below illustrates the limited risk and unlimited profit potential for this strategy:

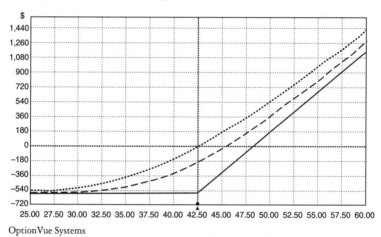

OptionVue Systems

Profit/Loss by Change in COMPANY E Common Price

As with the covered call strategy, the protective put investor retains all benefits of continuing stock ownership (dividends, voting rights, etc.) during the life of the put contract, unless he sells his stock. If there is a sudden, significant decrease in the market price of the underlying stock, a put owner has the luxury of time to react. Remember that the enemy of any option buyer is time. The time value portion of the protective put will steadily decrease with the passage of time, and this decrease accelerates as the option contract approaches expiration. But the investor employing the protective put is free to sell his

> The enemy of any option buyer is time.

stock and/or his long put at any time before it expires. For instance, if the investor loses concern over a possible decline in market value of his hedged underlying shares, the put option may be sold if it has market value remaining.

If the put option expires and has no value, no action needs to be taken; the investor will retain his stock. The only decision to be made is whether current market conditions still warrant protecting the stock. If so, simply buy another put farther out in time. The same technique of rolling options we described earlier with the covered call works just as well with the protective put. If the put closes in-the-money, the investor has two choices; he can exercise the right to sell the underlying stock at the strike price, or simply sell the put to close it, using the profits received from the put to offset any loss from the decline in the stock price.

The put does not have to be purchased at the same time as the stock. A common way to employ the protective put strategy is to buy a put after the stock price has already increased. If an investor has concerns about downside market risk or is afraid the stock price might fall back in the short-term, he can protect his unrealized profits using a put, without having to sell the stock. The put can always be sold later for what value it has when the uncertainty has passed.

It should be clear by now that you can profit using options whether the market is rising or falling. Investors tend to favor calls over puts, but puts can play as important a role as calls in a well-designed investment plan. Both calls and puts can be used purely for speculation, to generate income, or hedge the risk of stock positions. Let's take the time to review the four basic approaches to using options, since every strategy or combination grows out of these:

1. **Using calls when you are optimistic.** You believe the stock is going to rise, so you go long and buy call options. Other strategies include bull call spreads and covered calls when you own the stock.

2. **Using calls when you are pessimistic.** You believe the stock is going to remain within a trading range or fall in value, so you go short and sell bear call spreads.

3. **Using puts when you are optimistic.** If you believe the stock is going to rise, you can go short and sell naked puts; if the stock does rise, the put loses value and can be closed at a profit or allowed to

expire. This should be done only if you believe the stock would be a good value at the strike price. Remember, if the stock price falls below that, the put could be exercised and you would have to buy 100 shares at the strike price. Alternatively, you can initiate a bull put spread.

4. **Using puts when you are pessimistic.** If you believe a stock is going to fall in value, you can go long and buy puts or initiate a bear put spread. If you're right, the puts and/or spread will increase in value. If you own stock, you can also buy puts to protect against price drops on stocks in your portfolio.

In other words, there are a number of reasons to buy or sell options. Depending on the specific strategy, you can use them to speculate, produce income, or hedge risk. In some market conditions, buying or selling calls may not make as much sense as the corresponding use of puts. Thus, it is always wise to look at both sides—calls *and* puts—to find the strategies that will maximize your profits no matter what the overall market is doing. The beauty of options is that calls and puts in the right mix, or at the right time, can produce profits in any kind of market: up, down, or stagnant. There is always a strategy available that will produce profits. In the next chapter, we'll look at some advanced concepts and strategies that build on what we've learned in the last two chapters.

*Chapter 4*

# GETTING FANCY
## Advanced Concepts
## and Strategies

Options can free you from the uncertainties of traditional investing practices. Now that you have a firm grounding in the basics of options trading, we will introduce some of the more advanced concepts and strategies. While we won't go into these with as much detail as we did call and put options, it is important that you appreciate the vast array of possibilities options make available to you, and that you begin to familiarize yourself with some of the concepts that all successful option traders need to master.

We will begin by spending a little time looking at three important concepts in more detail: option pricing, volatility, and the Greeks. The section on option pricing will give you an overview of the factors that go into determining what the "fair value" of an option is. The section on volatility explains its importance, and also introduces you to the historical volatility charts that allow you to see the current volatility situation for a stock. The next concept we will look at is how option traders measure the sensitivity of an option's price to changes in various factors, and we will define common terms like Delta, Gamma, Theta, and Vega; otherwise known as the "the Greeks."

Finally, we will briefly look at a number of advanced strategies, explain how they are constructed, illustrate their risk/reward potential with a graph, and discuss the price expectations and market conditions they will be the most effective for. There are three general market directions:

> It is important to assess potential market movement when you are placing a trade.

up, down, and sideways. It is important to assess potential market movement when you are placing a trade. For example, if the market is going up, you can buy calls, sell puts, or buy the stock itself. Do you have any other choices? Yes. You can combine long and short options and the underlying stock in a wide variety of strategies. These strategies are designed to limit your risk, while taking advantage of specific price expectations and market conditions.

# Pricing Options—What's a "Fair" Price for an Option?

Fisher Black and Myron Scholes published an option pricing model, called the Black-Scholes formula, in 1973. This pricing model gave option traders the first practical way to quickly calculate what an option "should be" worth. While there have been improvements made over the years, some variation of this formula is still at the heart of most option pricing models today. We won't go into the mathematical details, but the main inputs into the model are Price (of the underlying stock), Time (left until the expiration date), Volatility (ideally, the stock's future volatility), the (risk-free) Interest Rate, and Dividends (paid over the time period of the option).

A good options analysis software program can incorporate all these variables into the pricing model and display theoretical prices for any option today and also in the future. Using the model, the software can construct graphs, like those you see in this book, that show the future behavior of any option trade at any point in the future. Unless you have options industry experience and are very good at doing math in your head, you want to use a computer to display these graphs and assist you in your decision-making process.

We have already looked at the impact the stock price and time have on the value of an option. How the price of the underlying stock affects an option's value is fairly straightforward. That the value of an option steadily decreases with the passage of time is also a relatively easy concept to understand, although you should be aware that option prices do not decrease in a linear fashion: the time premium erodes faster as the option nears the expiration date. Interest rates and dividends really have only a minor impact on the price of an option. But it is worth taking the time to look at the final input—Volatility—in a little more detail.

## Understanding Volatility—Of Vital Importance to Option Traders

It was mentioned earlier that volatility is often the most neglected of the major factors that influence option prices. We don't want to make that mistake here. Volatility is a vitally important consideration in options trading.

Every asset has quiet periods when its options are cheap, and volatile periods when its options are expensive. Professional option traders are always aware of current volatility levels in relation to their historical context. To gain that perspective, they view historical volatility charts. The figure below shows a sample chart:

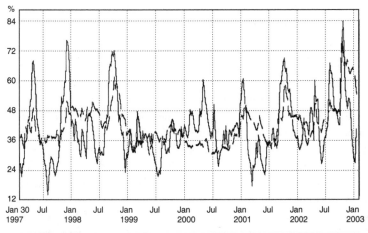

| Averages | 3 weeks | 6 weeks | 10 weeks | 1.5 years | 3 years | 4.5 years | 6 years |
|---|---|---|---|---|---|---|---|
| Statistical | 32.0% | 35.6% | 42.1% | 46.5% | 42.7% | 41.0% | 40.3% |
| Implied | 60.3% | 62.3% | 63.7% | 48.8% | 42.9% | 41.4% | 42.2% |

OptionVue Systems

The Volatility Chart displays two lines—one for statistical volatility (SV) and the other for implied volatility (IV). The solid SV line represents, at each point the actual volatility of the stock's daily price volatility. Statistical volatility is often referred to as "historical" volatility, but we prefer the term statistical since volatility charts contain historical data for both SV and IV. The dashed IV line represents, at each point, the average implied volatility for the stock. In other words, the SV line shows you the actual volatility of the stock, while the IV line shows you the volatility implied by the prices of the options of that stock. They should normally be fairly close together. If they are not, it would indicate the price of the options is not reflecting the actual volatility of the stock. At the bottom of the chart is a helpful table that summarizes the average SV and IV for various time periods.

Volatility Charts are also useful for determining what "normal" volatility is. This can help you profit when current volatility temporarily goes much higher or lower than in the past. It can also be useful for spotting patterns in volatility you can take advantage of. The price of a stock can range from zero to infinity. Volatility cannot range that far. The investor can always count on volatility eventually returning to normal levels after going to an extreme. This principle is called "the mean reversion tendency of volatility." It may take anywhere from days to months, but sooner or later volatility always comes back to middle ground.

Generally, implied volatility tends to increase as stock prices decline, and decreases as the stock prices rise. The reason this occurs is because falling stock prices mean greater uncertainty with regards to future risk. This leads to an institutional demand for insurance against future losses; meaning a higher demand for put options. This demand for puts drives implied volatility upward. On the other hand, increasing stock prices mean less uncertainty and subsequently less demand for put options resulting in lower implied volatility. This knowledge is very useful for option buyers. For instance, while the value of a call will increase with the stock price, the relationship between price and volatility means the call will lose some (sometimes a lot!) of its value due to the falling volatility. It is good news for put buyers, however, because puts will increase in value from the double effect of falling prices and increasing volatility.

At times, implied volatility and statistical volatility will be in close agreement, while at other times one soars way above the other. You should always be aware of current news on the stocks you are trading. Sometimes events can overwhelm historical volatility patterns. Be careful of situations where implied volatility is high and statistical volatility is extremely low. Find out if there is a takeover deal on the table. These deals often freeze the target company's stock in a narrow trading range for a while. Meanwhile, the options may maintain high premiums because of the possibility of a sudden change in the deal. In general, unusual events can be treacherous for options traders—so be careful!

## Understanding the Greeks—Measuring Your Risk

Because an option premium does not always appear to move in conjunction with the price of the underlying stock, it is important to understand the other factors that contribute to the movement of an option's price. Options traders often refer to the Delta, Gamma, Vega, and Theta of their positions. Collectively, these terms are known as the "Greeks," and they provide a way to measure the sensitivity of an option's price to different factors. These terms can be confusing and intimidating to new option traders, but broken down, they refer to simple concepts that can help you better understand the risk and potential reward of an option position. They cannot be looked up in your everyday option tables, but the best options software and online analysis sites automatically do the calculations and give you this information for every option and position you look at.

> An option premium does not always appear to move in conjunction with the price of the underlying stock.

Delta measures the sensitivity of an option's theoretical value to a change in the price of the underlying stock. It is represented by a number between 0 and 1, indicating how much the value of an option will increase when the stock price increases one dollar. Delta is a very important number to consider when constructing spreads and combinational positions. Call options have positive deltas and put options have negative deltas. At-the-money options generally have deltas of around .50. Deeper in-the-money options might have a delta of .80 or higher. Out-of-the-money options have deltas as small as .20 or less. Delta will change as the option becomes further in- or out-of-the money. When a stock option is deep in the money, it will begin to trade like the stock—moving dollar for dollar with the underlying stock, while the far out-of-the-money options don't move much.

Since Delta is such an important factor, the marketplace is interested in how Delta changes. **Gamma** measures the rate of change in the delta for each one-point increase in the underlying stock. It is a valuable tool in helping you forecast changes in the delta of an option or an overall position. Gamma is largest for the at-the-money options and gets progressively lower for both in- and out-of-the-money options. Unlike Delta, Gamma is always positive for both calls and puts. Delta and Gamma change constantly. The factors that affect Delta and Gamma are the same ones that affect an option's value including time, the price of the stock, and volatility.

The next Greek we will look at is **Vega,** which measures the sensitivity of the option's price to changes in implied volatility. Although implied volatility changes affect whole option chains, each option has its own Vega and will react by varying degrees. For instance, the impact of volatility changes is greater for at-the-money options than for the in- or out-of-the-money options. Longer-term options, especially LEAPS, have higher Vega, and thus their value is more sensitive to changes in volatility.

Finally, **Theta** is a measure of the time decay of an option. It is the dollar amount that an option will lose each day. For at-the-money options, Theta increases as an option approaches the expiration date. For in- and out-of-the-money options, theta decreases as an option approaches expiration. Theta is one of the most important concepts for a beginning option trader to understand because it explains what effect time has on the value of purchased or sold options. The further out in time you go, the smaller the time decay.

The Greeks can help you quantify the various risks of every trade you are considering, but it is important to realize that these numbers are strictly theoretical, and that the values are based on mathematical models. The Greeks provide an important measurement of the risks and potential rewards of an option position. Combining an understanding of the Greeks, with the insight that risk graphs provide, lets you take your options trading to another level.

A wide variety of option strategies exist which combine calls, puts, and the stock itself. These strategies exist, cover every possible scenario, and market environment. Some are created from options of just one type (calls or puts), while others use both in combination. Using a software program that models option price behavior, performance graphs allow us to evaluate very complicated option positions. It turns out that the risk/reward diagram of a complicated option position is just the sum of the graph of each component of the position. Thus, using performance graphs allows us to easily assess the potential of each strategy.

> A wide variety of option strategies exist which combine calls, puts, and the stock itself.

## Time Spreads—Combining Options with Different Expiration Dates

When you combine options of the same type, but with different expiration dates, it is referred to as a *calendar spread,* or *time spread.* We already mentioned one example earlier, when we discussed using LEAPS as a substitute for stock. That spread involved buying a LEAPS call and then selling a shorter-term call. Calendar spreads can also involve all short-term options. When the strike price of the two options is the same, it is called a *horizontal spread.* For example, you could buy a June call and sell a February call at the same strike price. Next is a risk graph that illustrates the potential risk/reward profile for this trade:

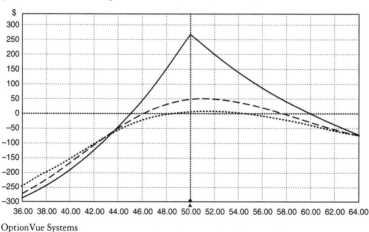

OptionVue Systems

Profit/Loss by Change in COMPANY F Common Price

As you can see, this trade profits when the stock price stays within a trading range at least until the short option expires. Your maximum possible profit occurs if the stock price finishes exactly at the strike price of the short option on expiration day. The precise shape and position of the "tent" depends on which strike price is used. In this trade you are hoping for two outcomes. First, that the short option expires worthless, or that you can close it at a profit. Second, that the later-expiring long option will be profitable before expiration. This strategy works if the time value disappears from the February call, and *then* the stock goes up before expiration of the June call. Of course, you can always close the entire position on the expiration date of the short option. Or you could "roll out," and sell another short option in the next expiration month.

A *diagonal spread* is a variation of the calendar spread in which both expiration date and strike price is different for long and short options. For example, you might decide to buy a June 50 call and sell a February 55 call. This trade would actually have a bullish profile, as illustrated by the performance graph:

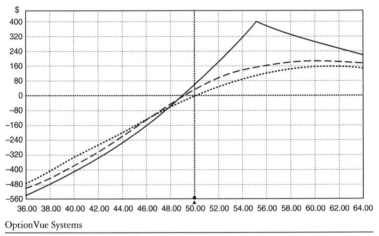

OptionVue Systems

Profit/Loss by Change in COMPANY F Common Price

The maximum profit possible is again if the stock price finishes at exactly the strike price of the short option on expiration day. However, you can clearly see that this is also a bullish directional bet. If the strike price drops, you will lose money. But if the stock price goes up, this trade is profitable over quite a wide range. The same strategy works just as well using puts for downside speculation. For example, you might buy a June 50 put and sell a February 45 put.

It should be pointed out that calendar spreads are very sensitive to changes in volatility. An increase in volatility could increase your profit substantially (the long, farther-out option will increase in value much more than your short nearby option). By the same token, a large drop in volatility could be devastating for these trades. So you should be careful not to enter this type of trade in a stock whose current implied volatility level is at a historical high.

# Ratio Spreads—Buying and Selling Unequal Amounts of Options

Up to this point, every spread strategy we have shown involved equal amounts of long and short options. But there are also ratio strategies, where the number of long options and short options are not identical. One useful ratio strategy is called the backspread. It is perfect for times when you expect a big price move, but at the same time know that you could be wrong and no move will develop.

A backspread is constructed by shorting a near-the-money option, and then buying a larger number of the same type of options (calls or puts) at a strike price farther out-of-the-money. The most common ratio is one by two, and you should try to choose the options in such a way that the option you're shorting brings in a credit that covers the cost of the options you're buying, resulting in no net cash flow, or even a small credit to your account. The risk graph of a call ratio backspread is illustrated in the figure on page 56.

The call ratio backspread is a hedged directional trade where we expect to profit from a strong upward movement, while hedging our downside. If the stock price does rise, you will profit from the upward price movement—similar to a long call position. If your expectations turn out to be wrong, and the market moves against you, this is positioned in such a way that you either do not lose, or may even move into a small profit zone.

Since you are net long options, the profit potential is unlimited. And since the sale of the more expensive options pays for the options you purchase, it costs you nothing if both legs expire worthless. The short leg of the backspread also helps reduce time decay as a worry. However,

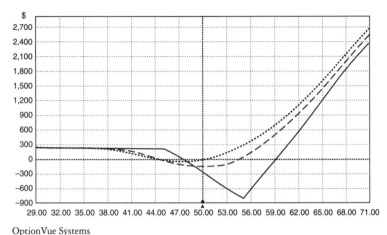

OptionVue Systems

Profit/Loss by Change in COMPANY F Common Price

there is a catch. There is a price zone where the backspread loses money, and it occurs if the stock moves in the desired direction by only a small amount. But it takes time for the maximum loss to develop, so that risk can be offset somewhat by using longer-term options. Then if the hoped-for big move fails to materialize in a reasonable amount of time, you can close the position for a small loss. Note that if you are bearish, backspreads can be constructed just as well with puts, and behave in a mirror image fashion to call backspreads.

## Combining Calls and Puts in a Single Strategy

Another option trading strategy is called the *straddle*. In this strategy, you combine both a call and a put on the same stock. Straddles can be sold for income, or bought for speculation. For example, let's say a stock is selling right now at $50 per share. You can sell the 50 call and the 50 put with the same expiration date, and get premium income of $3 on the call and also $3 on the put. You're up six dollars, receiving a credit to your account of $600. The stock could now move $6 in either direction by expiration day

> Straddles can be sold for income, or bought for speculation.

and you would break even. If the stock moved more than that either way, you would begin to lose money. Let's take a look at the risk/reward profile of a short straddle:

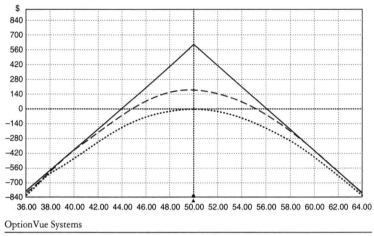

OptionVue Systems

Profit/Loss by Change in COMPANY G Common Price

Either or both of these options can be closed at a profit at any time. The big advantage to this trade is that time value comes out of both sides, allowing you to make a profit on both call and put when you close the position. That assumes, of course, that the stock price does not move too far in either direction. The short straddle is designed to generate income on stocks that stay in a very narrow trading range. The downside is that the margin required is likely to be very high.

In the previous example, the stock was right at the strike price, which is ideal for the straddle. That is because the entire premium of both the call and put sold was 100% time value. And all of that value is going to evaporate by expiration. The only value left on the expiration date will be any intrinsic value in either the call or the put. So in a straddle, you know that one side is going to expire worthless; as long as they have the same strike price, there cannot be intrinsic value in both the call *and* put on the same stock.

Considering the possibility that a stock could move significantly in one direction or another, you face a lot of risk in the short straddle. The premium you receive for selling both options mitigates risk only in a narrow trading range. So you expose yourself in the event of big price moves, either up or down. You could hedge that risk by buying options at a higher strike price on both sides and limit the potential loss; however, that would also decrease the potential profit from the credit you received when you sold the calls and puts originally. The short straddle can be a dangerous play, and you have to be ready to act quickly to defend your position.

Another way to use straddles is by going long. With a long straddle, you would *buy* calls and puts at the same strike price. While the risk of loss from price movement is less in the long straddle, it is also more difficult to produce a profit. The stock price must move enough in one direction or the other quickly enough to (1) offset the premium cost of *both* options and (2) to overcome the loss of value due to time decay. So using the same prices we used in the earlier example, if the total cost of a call and a put were 6 points, the stock price would have to move up or down $6 just to break even, and it has to move more than that to produce a profit. The performance graph of a long straddle is illustrated in the following figure:

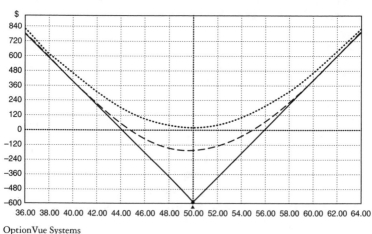

OptionVue Systems

Profit/Loss by Change in COMPANY G Common Price

The picture clearly shows how large a price move you need to make a profit on this trade. And if the stock price doesn't move, the relentless decrease in value due to time decay is illustrated by the other time lines.

The call and put do not necessarily have to be at the same strike price. You can adjust the risk/reward profile of the trade by adjusting the strike prices. When I first started trading options, if you bought or sold a call and a put at the same time it was always called a straddle, no matter what the strike prices. But as time went by it became common, if they had different strike prices, to call the trade a "strangle." The terms and expressions used in options trading do change over time.

But even these risk graphs don't show the whole story. When we discussed the effects of volatility on the value of an option earlier in this chapter, we mentioned that changes in volatility affect calls and puts in the same way. That means straddles are particularly sensitive to volatility. In fact some options traders, called volatility traders, use straddles to take advantage of expected changes in volatility, rather than price. An increase in volatility will help a long straddle, but hurt a short straddle, and visa versa. Thus, it is best to place long straddles on stocks that are at historically low levels of implied volatility (buy options when they're cheap), and sell short straddles on stocks at historically high levels of implied volatility (sell expensive options).

Now let's move on and look at two trades that combine calls, puts, *and* the stock: the covered combo and the collar trade.

## Buying Stock Cheaply with the Covered Combo

When options are very expensive, it makes sense to find a way to sell them. Covered writing is a good way, but you still lose if the stock price drops suddenly. What if you could buy some good stocks at a price below their current price levels? The covered combo lets you do just that.

The covered combo strategy consists of a covered call (long stock and short call) plus a short put. In addition to owning the stock, good premium is received by selling an out-of-the-money call to form the covered write, and then a put sold at a strike price where you would be willing to buy more shares of that stock. The short put is considered a naked option, and if the stock price falls below the strike price of the put, then you may be assigned and have to buy more shares. You simply need to be prepared to do this.

Since the covered combo has you selling options, this strategy is perfect for seasons of high option prices. Let's look at an example. With a stock currently trading at $50, we could sell a call option at the 60 strike for $3. That gives us 3 points of downside protection. In other words, the stock could drop to $47 before we incurred a loss. Then add to that the $4 credit available by selling a put at the strike price of 45. Regardless of where the stock price goes, the credit received from selling the put helps us buy the original 100 shares of stock for 4 points less. Considering the proceeds from the puts and the calls together, we're effectively buying the stock for $43. That's $7.00 below the current market value! The entire trade is pictured in the figure below:

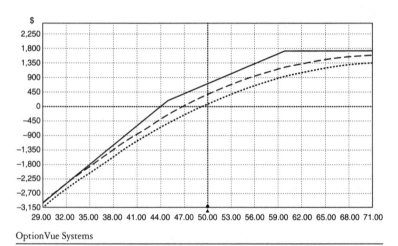

OptionVue Systems

Profit/Loss by Change in COMPANY G Common Price

If the stock does fall below $45, our (now) in-the-money put would probably be assigned and have to buy an additional 100 shares of stock at $45. So the first 100 shares cost $43 each and the second 100 cost us $45 each. That means we get 200 shares at an average price of $44. Not bad, considering the current price of the stock is $50!

So what's the catch? The catch is that if the stock continues to fall, we're losing $200 per point on our 200 shares of stock. If instead the stock soars, we can make $1,700 and no more, since our upside gains are capped by the short calls. So, in essence, our gain is limited but our potential loss is much higher, that is, any price below $35.50 results in a loss greater than $1,700.

## The Collar Trade—Hedging Your Stock for Little or Nothing Down

Buying a protective put is the simplest way to protect your gains in a stock without actually selling it. It has the advantage of letting you keep all the gains (minus the put premium paid) if the stock goes up, yet you're insured if the price drops. The downside to this strategy is cost. When the stock price goes up, investors tend to grumble about the expense of the put premiums. Over a long bull market, most investors simply stop buying the puts.

One way you can get around the expense of the downside protection is to use a collar trade. A collar trade is a hedge that confines your risk to a particular range. To construct a collar trade around a stock holding, you buy one put option for every 100 shares of stock you own to protect the stock from a drop in price. Then you sell call options (one call option for every 100 shares) to help pay for the puts. It is even possible on many stocks to create what is called a "costless" collar, where the money collected selling calls completely pays for buying the puts. What the collar trade does is lock you into a protected price band. You are protected if the stock falls below the strike price of the put, but forfeit any profits above the strike price of the call.

> Buying a protective put is the simplest way to protect your gains in a stock without actually selling it.

The collar trade can be placed at the same time you purchase the stock. It is also a very handy strategy if you have unrealized gains to protect. Let's look at an example with a stock currently trading at $55. You could purchase a July 45 put for $2.50, and sell a July 65 call for $2.50. The stock will cost you $5,500 for 100 shares, but the debit and credit from the two options cancel out, so the options cost you nothing. The risk graph of this trade is shown in the figure on page 62.

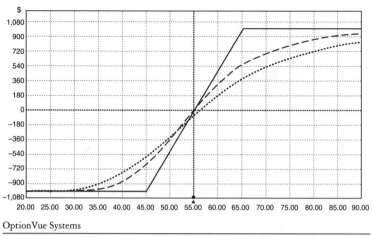

Profit/Loss by Change in COMPANY H Common Price

Now, a number of things could happen to the stock price between today and the July expiration.

- The stock price could remain between $45 and $65. In this case, both options will expire worthless and you still own 100 shares of stock. Since the options cost you nothing, you are no better or worse off than if you had simply bought the stock (although you got to sleep a little easier at night).

- The stock price could drop below $45 by the expiration date. In this case, you could lose up to $1,000 no matter how far the stock price drops. This is the "floor" established by the collar. For comparison, if the stock price drops to $40, you would have lost $1,500 if you only bought the stock. And with just the stock, your losses could continue to mount.

- The stock price could rise past $65. If this happens, your shares would be assigned at $65, no matter how high the stock price climbs. This will give you a profit of $1,000 for those 188 days, an 18% yield (35% annualized).

Can you make adjustments to increase the overall profitability of the position if the stock price falls dramatically? Of course! The adjustment is to sell the long put, buy back the short call, and then put a new collar on the stock. If the price of the underlying stock has decreased, a profit will be realized on the sale of the long put, and another profit realized on the purchase of the short call. The new collar will then continue to protect the position to the downside at the current price, and allow for profits if the stock were to head higher. The new collar will not require much, if any, additional cash from your account since selling the call finances the cost of the put for the new collar. It usually makes sense to look at doing an adjustment if the stock price has dropped by around 20% or so. What a powerful strategy! It allows you to lock in your profit, keep a long-term bullish position on, and have limited risk if the stock price collapses.

Option trading requires constant monitoring of the market and stock prices. Only by paying attention can you know when to act to maximize profits or minimize losses. Most option strategies—especially the combinations—cannot be opened and then ignored. And while it is possible to many things with options, that doesn't always mean they *should* be done. Complexity increases risk, and the more options you trade, the higher your commissions. And that could eat into your returns. The opportunities for using stock options present intriguing possibilities for (1) pure speculation, (2) generating income, and (3) hedging your risk. However, stock options are not the only options available. In the final chapter we will talk about how to use index options, options whose value is determined by a basket of stocks. Finally, we will discuss what some of your next steps might be as you start to trade options.

> Option trading requires constant monitoring of the market and stock prices.

*Chapter 5*

# CAPITAL PRESERVATION AND RULES FOR OPTIONS TRADING

In this final section we will explore index options, and how they can be used as part of your overall investment strategy. Then we proceed to give some suggestions on how to initially approach options trading. Different forms of options are used everyday. You have insurance on your house and car to protect your property from an unlikely catastrophe, for which you pay a small amount known as the premium. In the same way, investors can buy index options as insurance for stock holdings.

Capital preservation can be every bit as important as capital appreciation to your long-term investment returns. Sure, every investor would prefer to have consistent gains all the time, but events outside your control can cause a temporary drop in the value in your investments. Stock options allow you to hedge the risk of individual positions, while index options let you protect the value of your portfolio as a whole from unforeseen events.

## Index Options—A Useful Tool for Individual Investors

Prices of index options are based on a broad segment of the market, rather than on an individual stock. Stock options give you the right to buy or sell 100 shares of an individual stock. With index options, however, you cannot sell partial shares of hundreds of stocks, so "exercise" always means getting the difference in cash between current value and the strike price. But most of the same terms, strategies, and concepts we have already studied apply just as well to these instruments.

The concept of index options began in 1983, when the Chicago Board Options Exchange (CBOE) began offering options on an index of 100 stocks. This was called the Options Exchange Index, and is abbreviated OEX. Today, this index typically trades over 100,000 contracts worth over $20 million every day, and is still in the top ten of the most active options. Options are also available for the Dow Jones Industrial Index (DJX), the S&P 500 (SPX), the Philadelphia Semi-Conductor Index (SOX), the NASDAQ 100 (NDX), and dozens of others indexes tied to a particular market or sector.

Index options can be used to speculate on the future price movements of these markets, and most of the same strategies we went over with stock options can be applied. However, here we will focus on the use of index options to insure, or hedge, a portfolio against a broad market decline, while at the same time allowing that portfolio to participate in any market advance.

Institutions and mutual funds are the biggest customers for index options. They manage large diversified stock portfolios, and it is easier for them to purchase puts on an index or sector rather than purchasing them on hundreds of individual stocks. When analyzing how to hedge their risk, they must balance the cost of the strategy against their opinion of the market. Index puts are not cheap, so why are these managers willing to risk underperforming the market by 3% during a 90-day period (approximately a 13.2% annual rate)? The manager is willing to take that risk if he or she has a bearish view, and hopes to beat the market by profiting from the puts. The objective of the index option purchase is to limit or insure against portfolio losses.

> **Institutions and mutual funds are the biggest customers for index options.**

Volatility is an important measurement of risk, and index options have lower volatility than options on individual stocks. When you trade an index option, your profit or loss is not due to the movement of a single stock. The overall mix of the index determines its value, and this has a smoothing effect on price changes. The "averaging" effect on index options means that they tend to typically trade in a more narrow range (percentage-wise) than the range for many component stock options. Another feature that makes index options less volatile is that they are not as subject to company risk. A single event, such as a merger, or an unexpectedly low earnings report, will not affect the index as much as it does the individual stock. Just as a mutual fund delivers a more consistent return using a large portfolio of stocks, the index also benefits from this same diversifying effect relative to its component stocks.

## Using Index Options to Insure Your Portfolio

The technique of hedging your portfolio is straightforward. Find the index with the composition that most closely resembles your own portfolio, and then purchase out-of-the-money protective puts. But unlike stock options, where you know you need to purchase one put for every 100 shares of stock you own, your portfolio is unlikely to have precisely the same stocks as the index, and not in exactly the same proportion. There are measures like portfolio delta that allow you to come close, but hedging an individual portfolio is still a bit of an art. The unusual part of this strategy is your objective: purchase puts, and then hope they expire worthless!

Strange as it may sound, a portfolio manager actually hopes that his out-of-the-money put options expire worthless. After all, an honest homeowner does not hope that his house burns down so that the insurance policy will pay off. Similarly, a portfolio manager who buys out-of-the-money puts doesn't hope the market declines so that his portfolio will decrease in value by less than the overall market. This is a hard concept for many investors to understand. But an experienced money manager recognizes there are times when a sharp market correction, while not expected, has a high enough probability of occurring to justify the expenditure of 1% to 3% of the portfolio on out-of-the-money puts for 1 to 3 months of insurance.

You can also use index options to insure other positions, to a degree. For example, if you have invested part of your portfolio in shares of a mutual fund, you could buy index option puts to protect your shares in the event of a downturn in overall value. This assumes that (1) the index you select approximates the equity holdings of the mutual fund and that (2) you believe the market is heading upward, but you recognize the possibility that your timing is off. The match might not be exact, but the strategy has a specific purpose: to anticipate and protect against *broad* declines of the type we have all seen in recent years. Markets do tend to move generally in the same direction, so that stocks—even those whose individual fundamentals are strong—decline when the overall market does. By the same argument, a strong bull market tends to pull most stocks in an upward direction, including under-performers, at least to some extent.

## Using Index Options for Speculation and Diversification

Index options can also be used for speculation. Here they offer the advantage of diversification, helping you to avoid the all too common mistake of simply picking the wrong stock. It is possible to time your decision well but pick the wrong equity. So while a sector might perform strongly as a group, the one exception could be the stock in which you invest all your capital! Diversification has been the major appeal of mutual funds for equity investors; and it works equally well for option investors or speculators. Some people think that owning shares of five different stocks is enough diversification; but in a weak market, all five might fall in value. Other investors believe that a sensible alternative is buying shares of mutual funds. However, mutual funds have a number of drawbacks:

> Index options can also be used for speculation.

1. **Management charges a fee.** Every mutual fund charges an annual fee, a percentage of the portfolio that goes to management salaries. This fee is charged whether share values rise or fall. With index options, you pay a transaction fee on both sides, but other than that, you keep all your profits.

2. **A Load might apply as well.** Many mutual funds are also subject to a load fee, as much as 8% of all the capital you invest. So for every $100 you put in, you have only $92 at work. The load fee discounts your investment, even when the fund performs poorly. Why pay a sales commission? If you're sophisticated enough to consider options, you don't need to use a mutual fund salesman to tell you where to

deposit your funds. If you must invest in a fund, use a no-load; they have historically performed on a par with the load funds, and you don't need to support a salesperson in addition to putting your capital at risk.

3. **You're still putting capital at risk without leverage.** When you buy shares of mutual funds you're buying at 100% levels, with no leverage. That means that *all* of your capital is at risk at full price. So if the value of the fund falls, you have lost money. In recent years, millions of investors have found themselves invested in funds whose current market value is far below their invested value. They either sell at a loss or sit tight and wait for the market to turn around—just to get back to their starting point. With index options, this problem is avoided because your only risk (in long positions, at least) is the amount of the premium paid, which is a fraction of the index values you control.

4. **Equity diversification can work against you.** One of the "dirty little secrets" on Wall Street is that diversification is not always a profitable tactical move. If the overall market performs poorly, even a well-diversified portfolio is likely to lose value. For an investor who does not understand how the market works, diversification (using mutual funds) provides some comfort. However, only a small portion of all equity funds actually beat the overall market. The impressive long-term returns claimed in mutual fund brochures are generally the result of reinvested dividends and capital gains, not because the fund has some great insight into which stocks to buy.

> Diversification is not always a profitable tactical move.

As a general rule, investors tend to think only in terms of timing for upward price movement. Everyone wants to buy low and sell high. But whether you use individual stock options or index options, don't overlook the importance of the put. If the market trend is downward, you can make as much money, or more, buying puts than you can when you buy calls hoping for a reversal in price movement. Most investors are incurable optimists, and tend to think of puts only for insurance or as part of other strategies designed to profit when prices go up.

# Conclusion: Now You Can Answer the Questions "Why Options?"

> It is important to understand both the risk and potential rewards of any option trade *before* you enter it.

We started this book asking the question: Why options? We have tried to answer that question using specific examples, and hopefully you are beginning to feel comfortable with the idea of using options in your daily investment routine. Options open up a lot of possibilities; opportunities for leveraged speculation, conservative income generation, and also portfolio insurance. So why is it that options often are considered riskier than stocks? The difference, of course, is time. Because options often expire worthless, you can easily lose *all* your investment. That is why it is important to understand both the risk and potential rewards of any option trade *before* you enter it, and today's technology actually allows every trader, private or professional, to evaluate a proposed option trade with amazing speed and relative ease.

Computer software that models the behavior of option trades can help tremendously. It is entirely possible to trade options without the help of computers and financial software. But why would you, when you'd be at such a disadvantage? Options analysis software does all the calculations for you, and displays risk graphs that let you quickly make essential trading decisions. There is a significant benefit to seeing all the potential outcomes graphically, including how a position will respond to movement in the stock price, to time decay, and to changes in implied volatility. Certainly the people you are trading against will be using it. Trading options profitably, even with the proper tools, can sometimes be difficult; why deliberately try to make it harder?

One of the important differences between options and stocks is that options are really contracts. They always have two sides, so for every call or put purchased, there is someone else selling it. Options are a zero-sum game. That means that an option buyer's gain is the option seller's loss, and vice versa (ignoring commissions). Because of this, any payoff diagram of the dollar return from buying an option must be the mirror image of the seller's profit and loss profile.

# The Need for Vigilance

Perhaps the most difficult aspect of buying and selling options is self-discipline. If you do not set your own policies and trading rules regarding when to close positions, how to reduce risks, or exactly what you hope to achieve, then it will be difficult to profit from trading options. The successful options trader is one who understands the importance of self-discipline and has the ability to open and close positions in accordance with predefined trading rules, even when you are tempted to do otherwise. The fast-changing nature of the options market, ever-looming expiration dates, and the different factors that affect the time value of an option all require that you be aware of how time works for or against you in order to maximize your profits.

> The most difficult aspect of buying and selling options is self-discipline.

# Two Policies

You need to establish policies in two broad areas: First, know why you are using options, and second, know your exit point!

Initially, understand the purpose of your option trading. Are you using options for leveraged speculation? If so, then you better have proper market timing tools to trigger precise entries and exits. Are you using options for added income from your stock holdings? Then know which of your stocks have options with high implied volatility levels so that the option selling is worth the effort. Finally, you might use options as insurance against investment loss. If so, then strongly consider the collar strategy that is used by countless institutions every day. In short, understand what category of option trader you fall under.

The second policy area involves a specific exit strategy. You need to think about possible scenarios and decide—in advance—when you will close a position. You could hold options until expiration day or exit the week prior. If you have bought an option, you should identify a profit sell point as well as a loss bail out point. You might determine to sell if you double your money (on the upside) or lose one-third (on the downside). Rules like that, no matter what the specific exit points, define a specific event where action should be taken.

Risk exposure is yet another issue to consider. For example, let's say you are short calls and expiration day is near. The stock is one point out of the money, and the option is now worth only 10 cents. Should you wait for expiration and, considering that the option is close to the money, take the risk the stock will jump before the option expires? For a dime per contract, it might be prudent to just close out the position, just in case the stock did rise at the last minute.

If you follow your rules and resist the temptation to make exceptions, then you will most likely succeed. Without standards for getting out at the right time, you would certainly fail. Neither stocks nor options can be treated as separate parts of the portfolio. They should work together. This is the advantage to options: They are useful as a part of your overall investment strategy.

## The Next Steps

Where should you go from here? You should continue your education and begin to assemble the trading tools you need. Books, classes, option trading workshops and specialized options Web sites all have their place in your trading education. And it is nearly impossible nowadays to trade without access to a computer, including software for analyzing trades and obtaining current market data. The goal of your financial education should not be to reach a certain point. Rather it is a journey, and even the most experienced traders need to keep adding to their investment knowledge. Also consider getting a broker that specializes in options. You can trade options in most equity accounts at the major brokerage firms (with some additional paperwork and a statement confirming you understand the risks associated with options), but firms specializing in options can also offer you tools and knowledge that will help you in your trading.

All option trades are built on the foundations we have outlined in this guide. Be sure to take your time when thinking about how to trade an option, or understand a certain spread trade. Paper trading (without putting actual money at risk) is one way to begin gaining experience and learning how options behave. Once you master the concepts and strategies for options, you should do well when you begin to actually trade them. Enjoy the challenges, the rewards, and the journey!

*Appendix*

# KEY POSITIONS

## Long Calls

Bullish
Limited Risk, Unlimited Potential Gain
Definition:  Buy In-, At-, or Out of-the-Money Call
Time Decay Effect:  Negative
Increasing Implied Volatility Effect:  Positive

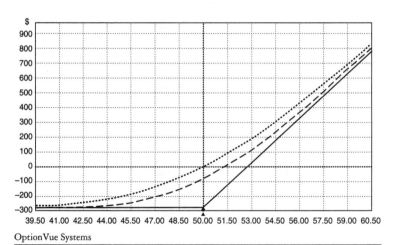

OptionVue Systems

Profit/Loss by Change in XYZ Common Price

## Bull Call Spread (Vertical Debit Spread)

Bullish

Limited Risk, Limited Potential Gain

Definition: Buy In-, At-, or Out of-the-Money Call; Sell Farther Out-of-the-Money Call

Time Decay Effect: Negative Below Midpoint Between the Two Strikes, Positive Otherwise

Increasing Implied Volatility Effect: Limited Effect

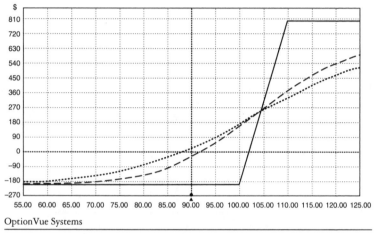

OptionVue Systems

Profit/Loss by Change in COMPANY A Common Price

## Covered Call (Covered Write)

Bullish

Limited but Large Risk (Stock Price to $0), Limited Potential Gain

Definition: Long Stock; Sell In-, At-, or Out of-the-Money Call

Time Decay Effect: Positive

Increasing Implied Volatility Effect: Negative

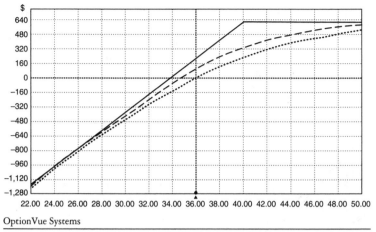

Profit/Loss by Change in COMPANY B Common Price

## Bear Call Spread (Vertical Credit Spread)

Bearish

Limited Risk, Limited Potential Gain

Definition: Sell In-, At-, or Out of-the-Money Call; Buy Farther Out of-the-Money Call

Time Decay Effect: Positive

Increasing Implied Volatility Effect: Negative

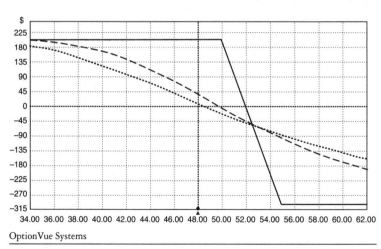

Profit/Loss by Change in COMPANY C Common Price

## Long Put

Bearish

Limited Risk, Limited (Stock Price to $0) But Large Potential Gain

Definition: Buy In-, At-, or Out-of-the-Money Put

Time Decay Effect: Negative

Increasing Implied Volatility Effect: Positive

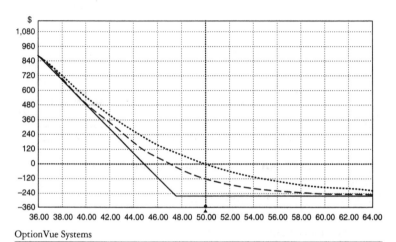

OptionVue Systems

Profit/Loss by Change in XYZ Common Price

## Bear Put Spread (Vertical Debit Spread)

Bearish

Limited Risk, Limited Potential Gain

Definition: Buy In-, At-, or Out-of-the-Money Put; Sell Farther Out-of-the-Money Put

Time Decay Effect: Negative Above Midpoint between the Two Strikes, Positive Otherwise

Increasing Implied Volatility Effect: Limited

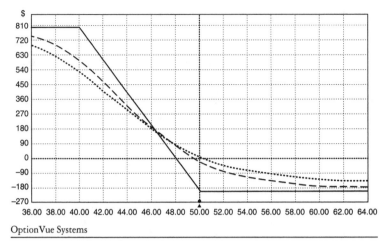

Profit/Loss by Change in COMPANY D Common Price

### Naked Put Sale

Bullish
Limited Risk, Limited (Stock Price to $0) But Large Risk
Definition: Sell In-, At-, or Out-of-the-Money Put
Time Decay Effect: Positive
Increasing Implied Volatility Effect: Negative

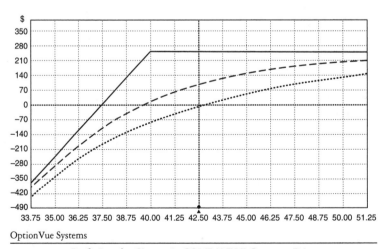

Profit/Loss by Change in COMPANY E Common Price

## Bull Put Spread (Vertical Credit Spread)

Bullish

Limited Risk, Limited Potential Gain

Definition: Sell In-, At-, or Out-of-the-Money Put; Buy Farther Out-of-the-Money Put

Time Decay Effect: Positive

Increasing Implied Volatility Effect: Limited Effect

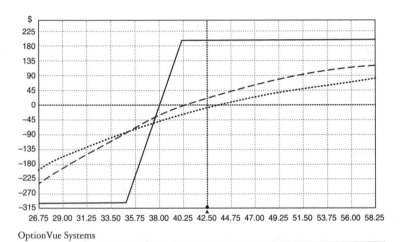

OptionVue Systems

Profit/Loss by Change in COMPANY E Common Price

## Protective Put

Bullish

Limited Risk, Unlimited Potential Gain

Definition: Long Stock; Buy In-, At-, or Out-of-the-Money Put

Time Decay Effect: Negative

Increasing Implied Volatility Effect: Positive

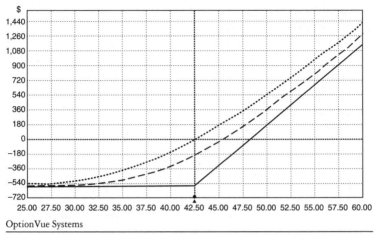

Profit/Loss by Change in COMPANY E Common Price

## Horizontal Debit Spread (Calendar Spread or Time Spread)

Neutral, Bullish, or Bearish, Depending on What Strike is Used

Limited Risk, Limited Potential Gain

Definition: Sell In-, At-, or Out-of-the-Money Call or Put; Buy the
  Same Type of Option at the Same Strike but in a Farther Out Month

Time Decay Effect: Positive

Increasing Implied Volatility Effect: Positive

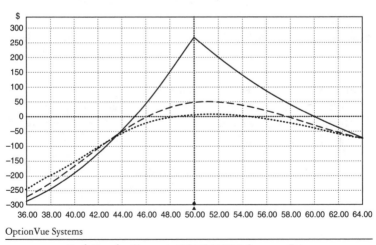

Profit/Loss by Change in COMPANY F Common Price

## Diagonal Debit Spread (Diagonal Calendar Spread)

Bullish or Bearish, Depending on Type and Strikes

Limited Risk, Limited Potential Gain

Definition: Sell In-, At-, or Out-of-the-Money Call or Put; Buy the
Same Type of Option at a *Different* Strike and in a Farther Out
Month

Time Decay Effect: Positive

Increasing Implied Volatility Effect: Positive

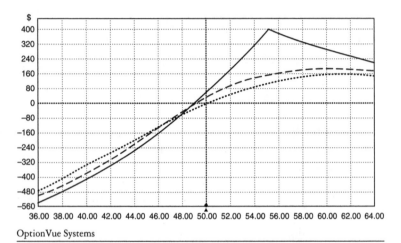

OptionVue Systems

Profit/Loss by Change in COMPANY F Common Price

## Backspread (Ratio Spread)

Bullish or Bearish, Depending on Type of Option and Level of Credit
(if Any)

Limited Risk, Limited Potential Gain

Definition: Sell In-, At-, or Out-of-the-Money Call or Put; Buy
Multiple Number of Farther Out of-the-Money Options of Same
Type, Preferably for a Net Credit

Time Decay Effect: Negative

Increasing Implied Volatility Effect: Positive

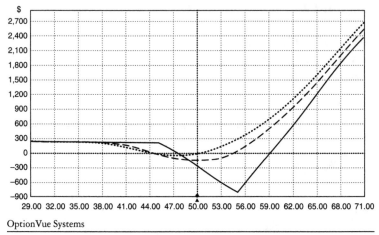

Profit/Loss by Change in COMPANY F Common Price

## Short Straddle

Neutral

Unlimited Risk, Limited Potential Gain

Definition: Sell At-the-Money Call and At-the-Money Put

Time Decay Effect: Positive

Increasing Implied Volatility Effect: Negative

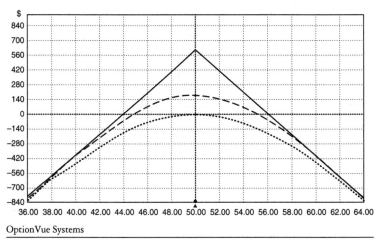

Profit/Loss by Change in COMPANY G Common Price

## Long Straddle

Neutral

Limited Risk, Unlimited Potential Gain

Definition: Buy At-the-Money Call and At-the-Money Put

Time Decay Effect: Negative

Increasing Implied Volatility Effect: Positive

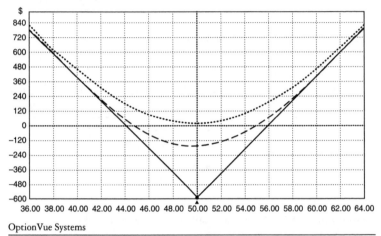

OptionVue Systems

Profit/Loss by Change in COMPANY G Common Price

## Covered Combo

Bullish

Limited (Stock to $0) But Large Risk, Limited Potential Gain

Definition: Long Stock; Sell Out-of-the-Money Call; Sell Out-of-the-Money Put

Time Decay Effect: Positive

Increasing Implied Volatility Effect: Negative

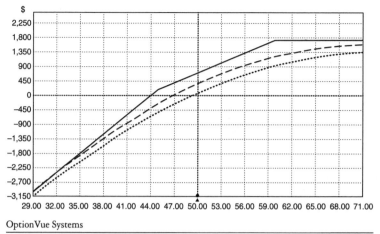

OptionVue Systems

Profit/Loss by Change in COMPANY G Common Price

## Collar Trade

Bullish

Limited Risk, Limited Potential Gain

Definition: Long Stock; Buy At- or Out-of-the-Money Call; Sell At- or
Out-of-the-Money Put

Time Decay Effect: Positive with Upward Price Movement, Negative
Otherwise

Increasing Implied Volatility Effect: Limited

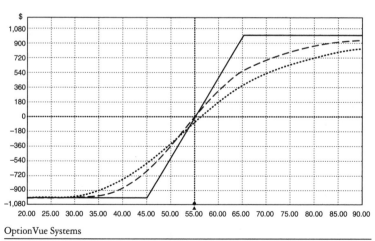

OptionVue Systems

Profit/Loss by Change in COMPANY H Common Price

# Resource Guide

## Recommended Reading

### Spread Trading: Low Risk Strategies for Profiting from Market Relationships
*by Howard Abell*

Cash in on the amazing opportunities this popular hedge technique offers. Howard Abell shows you how to capitalize on recognized relationships in the commodity and financial markets. You'll get on-target analysis of historical spread relationships, step-by-step details on time proven strategies, and in-depth interviews with top spread traders.

$40.00                                        Item #T184X-1161013

### Profit with Options: Essential Methods for Investing Success
*by Larry McMillan*

Finally—the book option traders and McMillan fans have been waiting for. *Profit with Options: Essential Methods for Investing Success* is a powerful new guide that allows every investor to learn about options by benefiting from the wealth of knowledge and years of experience of a true options expert.

$39.95                                           Item #T184X-84660

### Big Trends in Trading: Strategies to Master Major Market Moves
*by Price Headley*

Big trading profits are achieved when you identify the big market trends—and ride them for all they're worth. Now, BigTrends.com founder Price Headley provides a playbook that shows you how to spot stocks ready to take off—and strategies for reaping consistent rewards in all market climates. Emphasizing the aggressive use of options, his methods cover all the major market indicators. Get ready to post some big returns, when you start using the BigTrends method for finding market winners.

$39.95            Item #T184X-17554

### The Four Biggest Mistakes in Option Trading
*by Jay Kaeppel*

Earn huge profits in options trading by avoiding the 4 most common—and most costly—mistakes the majority of traders make. System and software developer Jay Kaeppel shows you how to avoid the most common pitfalls option traders encounter that cause them to lose money in the long run.

$19.95            Item #T184X-8471

### Trading Classic Chart Patterns
*by Thomas N. Bulkowski*

From the author of the Encyclopedia of Chart Patterns comes his latest work, *Trading Classic Chart Patterns,* a groundbreaking primer on how to trade the most popular stock patterns. Written for the novice investor but containing techniques for the seasoned professional, this comprehensive guide includes easy-to-use performance tables supported by statistical research.

$69.95            Item #T184X-85081

### The Conservative Investor's Guide to Trading Options
*by Leroy Gross*

Don't be mislead by the title! It's one of the most widely read books covering safe yet profitable options strategies for more conservative players. Concise and readable, this new work explores numberous safe, low risk options strategies and ways to use options as a hedging tool.

$34.95            Item #T184X-10267

# Option Trading Courses

## Mastering Option Trading Volatility Strategies
*with Sheldon Natenberg*

Join the ranks of the most successful option traders by mastering the key concept affecting option pricing—volatility. The world's most acclaimed volatility expert and "Trader's Hall of Fame" award winner Sheldon Natenberg provides a powerful, nontechnical, step-by-step workshop for understanding why and how volatility plays such a critical role in options trading.

$99.00                                          VHS Item #T184X-982362
                                                DVD Item #T184X-982367


## LEAPS Trading Strategies: Powerful Techniques for Options Trading Success
*with Marty Kearney*

Learn powerful, proven LEAPS trading strategies from a leading expert. The Options Industry Council's popular instructor, Marty Kearney of the Chicago Board Options Exchange, presents an in-depth LEAPS trading workshop that covers it all, from the basics to more advanced techniques for incorporating LEAPS into your overall investment strategy.

$99.00                                          VHS Item #T184X-982460
                                                DVD Item #T184X-982463


## Becoming a Disciplined Trader: Techniques for achieving peak trading performance
*with Ari Kiev*

Every trader has, at some point, let emotions guide their trading—usually resulting in costly results. The most successful traders will even tell you that the discipline they were forced to embrace as a result, was the key to their future trading success. Now, *Trading to Win* author Dr. Ari Kiev brings his personal coaching workshop into your own home, so you can develop the skills it takes to be a cool, collected, and consistently successful trader.

$64.95                                          VHS Item #T184X-982363
                                                DVD Item #T184X-982370

# Important Web Sites

- **www.cboe.com**

  Founded in 1973, the Chicago Board Options Exchange is the world's largest options exchange and the creator of listed options.

- **www.optionvue.com**

  OptionVue Systems and its affiliate, OptionVue Research, provide professional and individual traders with award-winning options analysis software, web-based tools, education programs, and advisory services.

- **www.888options.com**

  The Options Industry Council (OIC) is a nonprofit association dedicated to educating investors about the benefits and risks of exchange-traded equity options.

- **www.ptisecurities.com**

  PTI Securities and Futures understands the needs of traders and delivers full service at competitive rates. At PTI our brokers work as a trading team—YOUR trading team!

- **www.marketwise.com**

  The premier trading school focuses on equities, options, and futures for both retail and institutional traders.

# Publications of Interest

- OptionVue Newsletter
  Editors, Jim Graham and Steve Lentz
  **www.optionvueresearch.com**

- The Option Advisor
  Editor, Bernie Schaffer
  **www.schaeffersresearch.com**

- Daily Option Strategist
  Editor, Larry McMillan
  **www.optionstrategist.com**

- BigTrends.com Newsletter
  Editor, Price Headley
  **www.bigtrends.com**

- *SFO Magazine*
  **www.sfomag.com**

- *Active Trader Magazine*
  **www.activetradermag.com**

# Free 2 Week Trial Offer for U.S. Residents From Investor's Business Daily:

**I**NVESTOR'S BUSINESS DAILY will provide you with the facts, figures, and objective news analysis you need to succeed.

*Investor's Business Daily* is formatted for a quick and concise read to help you make informed and profitable decisions.

# About the Authors

**Jim Graham** is presently the Senior Analyst for OptionVue Research. Jim conducts intensive market research and provides daily commentary on the company's trading portfolio. Previously, he served as Product Manager for OptionVue Systems, a leading developer of options analysis software.

Jim worked in Corporate Banking at First National Bank of Chicago, specializing in loan syndications and asset sales as well as asset-backed finance. He also spent five years in the Securities and Commodities division of First Chicago Capital Markets, working with Broker-Dealers, Hedge Funds, and other securities firms to meet their financing and settlement needs. During this period, he also focused on developing new loan, collateral analysis, and broker settlement systems.

Jim has authored documentation and articles on options trading which have explored how to effectively use options analysis and trading software to increase the probability of long-term success in options trading.

He earned his B.A. in Economics from Lake Forest College, Lake Forest, Illinois, and has conducted graduate-level business study at the University of Chicago.

**Steve Lentz** is the Director of Education and Research for OptionVue Research, Inc. In addition to developing curriculum and teaching courses on options strategies, trading, and software, Steve conducts continuing research on the use of options as part of a profitable trading approach. Previously, he served OptionVue Systems as a Product Consultant.

An active trader in equities, futures, and options, Steve has studied the markets for many years and writes continually on topics ranging from beginner-level trading concepts through advanced technical analysis. Many of his articles are published in the OptionVue Informer, where he once served as editor.

Prior to joining OptionVue, Steve operated an independent real estate appraisal business in Southern California. He holds Bachelor of Arts degree in Economics from UCLA.